REINVENTING CULTURAL ARCHITECTURE

REINVENTING CULTURAL ARCHITECTURE

A radical vision by

OPEN

Catherine Shaw

RIZZOLI
NEW YORK

New York · Paris · London · Milan

CONTENTS

p.24

01

UCCA DUNE ART MUSEUM

p.60

02

TANK SHANGHAI

p.98

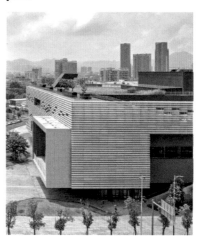

03

PINGSHAN PERFORMING ARTS CENTRE

FOREWORD

Aric Chen

General and Artistic Director
Het Nieuwe Instituut, Rotterdam,
Netherlands

When Li Hu and Huang Wenjing founded OPEN Architecture in Beijing, during the city's 2008 Summer Olympics, the Chinese capital was in the midst of a euphoria that—with its Bird's Nest stadium, Water Cube aquatics centre, cantilevered CCTV tower, and other (mostly foreign-designed) architectural acrobatics—trumpeted the country as a playground for architects from around the world.

Nearly fifteen years later, the reputation still sticks, and design firms from abroad continue to churn out large-scale projects throughout the country. But the frisson is gone. By and large, foreign architects are no longer producing their most compelling work for China—or perhaps China has lost its appetite for the anything-goes frenzy of the past. Whatever the case, the more significant, and perhaps substantial, phenomenon these days is the emergence of a generation of now mid-career Chinese architects who have been re-establishing the field, and its social and cultural potential, on new terms.

OPEN is one of the leading protagonists in this shift towards an architecture that responds more profoundly to China's needs, circumstances, and possibilities. Their work, like the museums and hybrid theatre-library profiled in this book, exemplifies the notion that, at its most consequential, built form is the reification of context in all senses: social, cultural, and systemic, as well as physical, urban, and formal. It highlights the shortcomings of simply transplanting models—whether imposed from abroad or, in a top-down system, from above—to local conditions that call for more localised responses.

Indeed, it's no accident that Li Hu and Wenjing chose OPEN for their name. On the one hand, the studio takes an approach that is highly flexible, easily adapting to China's famously frenetic pace of change (and often last-minute decision-making), while, at the same time, insisting on breaking open rigid typologies and mindsets in order to facilitate openness in social practice and use. That is to say, OPEN gives architecture a reason for existing beyond the sometimes heavy-handed political, financial, and bureaucratic agendas that still dominate architectural production in China. In so doing, the architects are not fighting those agendas per se, but rather coaxing them towards social, cultural, natural, and programmatic ones as well.

In this sense, OPEN represents the immense influence that architects can still wield in China as members of a profession who often do not respond to client briefs so much as they actually shape them. As one sees with the projects in this book, Chinese architects are frequently presented with vague directives that present challenges—but also opportunities. And so, a museum commission can become an excuse to also build a park, as with Tank Shanghai. Or a design for a school, as with the Shanghai Qingpu Pinghe International School, presents a chance to reformulate the country's standard educational typology: from a monolith adjacent to a vast (usually empty) field, to a variegated campus that articulates the facets of a more rounded education, including a theatre-library—the Bibliotheatre—that doubles as a centre for the wider community. Indeed, 'open' also describes the possibilities that building in China still offers.

Sometimes, the logic is counterintuitive for those who are not familiar with it. Several years ago, I wrote an article about OPEN's UCCA Dune Art Museum for an American magazine. When the editor in New York sent back her queries, she asked whether there was any controversy, as there surely must have been, surrounding its construction within sand dunes—an environmentally protected landscape in the United States. In fact, it was by embedding the building within the dune, which would have otherwise been demolished, that OPEN was actually saving it.

UCCA Dune also marked the beginning of a remarkable new thread in OPEN's work: the concretisation, literally, of natural and physical phenomena through architecture. In this project, and subsequent ones, the studio has shown agility—not just in approach, but also in built form—through extraordinarily sculptural buildings shaped by sand and, in the case of the Chapel of Sound and Sun Tower, acoustics and solar cycles respectively.

Indeed, context is all-encompassing and, somewhat ironically, it is both local and universal at the same time. OPEN is a studio that has thrived in the Chinese context because it understands how to use the system to architectural advantage while, importantly, equating architectural advantage with social benefit. This is no small achievement in a discipline that can be stubbornly insular and self-referential. In this way, OPEN offers broad lessons about specificity—about how a methodology of localisation is of global significance, and about how architecture can still find new relevance and meaning wherever sound travels and the sun shines.

INTRODUCTION

The first OPEN building I experienced was the UCCA Dune Art Museum. There was something captivating about the collection of modest, primordial cave-like galleries, hidden within a fragile sand dune on a remote beach in northeast China. The natural harmony of scale, organic form, and materiality felt calm and elegant, and intuitive to move through. I immediately noticed how the powerful architecture shaped the whole experience without overwhelming or dominating the art.

I was intrigued by the ingenious blurring of learned boundaries between architecture, landscape, and art, as well as the careful materiality and curves of monolithic concrete, and the museum's fundamental connection to the site. As soon as I returned to Beijing, I sought out the architects Li Hu and Huang Wenjing. Both had studied in the United States, gaining their early design experience at acclaimed New York firms Steven Holl Architects and Pei Cobb Freed & Partners respectively, before returning to China where they founded OPEN. Since then, they have assiduously built a body of work that is innovative in its functionality and a world away from the conventions of architectural and cultural interpretations.

This book introduces six recent and very different cultural projects, ranging from the hidden, small, and remote to the monumental urban. It includes new-builds as well as repurposed buildings, and designs for both public and private clients. No project is like another, although all are egalitarian, versatile places for relaxation and socialisation as much as they are for stimulation and inspiration. At the core of each project lies the conviction that a building should be more than a repository of culture, but must also play an important role in community life.

Each chapter explains the inspiration and creative thinking behind its project, and is illustrated with hand-drawn sketches, diagrams, plans, and photographs that highlight the realities of designing for the fast-changing cultural landscape of modern-day China. The book also includes a foreword by Aric Chen, General and Artistic Director Het Nieuwe Instituut, Rotterdam, and a conversation between the architects and Martino Stierli, the Philip Johnson Chief Curator of Architecture and Design at The Museum of Modern Art (MoMA), New York, whose support for OPEN stems from his personal experience and appreciation of the UCCA Dune Art Museum and Tank Shanghai projects. A building model of the former is part of the MoMA collection.

Li Hu and Wenjing believe that architecture must belong to its location and time, and that it should give people agency to use their cultural spaces in a way that they like and understand. In China, that calls for a delicate balance between firmness and flexibility, focusing on the main design objective while keeping an open mind, and being prepared to change—sometimes to pivot—at the very last minute. Each design project was a test of knowing how and when to maximise the opportunities that a fluid design and construction environment can provide, and when to defend the integrity and essential details of a design concept.

I can't remember exactly when we decided to write this book together, but, as I was leaving their office in Beijing after our first meeting, I do remember spotting their otherworldly model for the Chapel of Sound. I was intrigued by how the monastic void within a meteor-like structure would develop into both a performing arts centre and space for calm contemplation. We kept in touch and, after a while, it simply felt natural to collect their intriguing stories and to try and provide an insight, from their perspective, into the unusual challenges and opportunities of designing and building in China today. For the past few decades, Chinese architecture has been viewed as a playground for international architects. While this is still true to some extent, the stereotype distracts from the far more exciting story: the growing number of young Chinese architects—a counteraction to the influx of international designers—who are bringing a spirit of new thinking to the built landscape of China, and abroad, with more nuanced and relevant designs. The audience, too, has changed, developing expectations for contemporary culture at both a local and national level.

Over the past year, throughout the COVID-19 pandemic, Li Hu, Wenjing, and I have talked for hundreds of hours about their projects, vision, and hopes. It has been a strange time to focus on cultural architecture while so many museums around the world have been closed. In some ways, this has provided an unprecedented opportunity to step back and think more objectively about the function and relevance of cultural spaces around the world ... to ask ourselves, what works and what needs to change? How does a museum or cultural centre stay relevant? And what do we really miss when we can't access culture in physical spaces?

This time of confinement has also given us the opportunity to look at how daily life—from the traditional library, office, and shopping mall to the home—has been radically disrupted. Is it now time for us to reconsider how we face and absorb culture? This goes beyond adding a café and museum shop. Both are always welcome in any cultural building, but they are not bold innovations, especially when the entrance, galleries, and theatres remain fixed in traditional linear typologies, and while so many people perceive them as the preserve of a privileged or intellectual elite. Indeed, some of the world's best-known museums were intentionally designed to be visually impactful, yet can be quite intimidating, especially to an inexperienced audience, and, over the past few years, leading museums such as MoMA have made efforts to become more thoughtful and inclusive.

This is part of what makes OPEN's work so distinctive. Apart from the technical rigour and the poetry of their structures, Li Hu and Wenjing are constantly thinking about the realities of life in one of the world's most dynamic, fast-paced economies. They do not shy away from the essential question of what architecture is. Or what culture is. Or what museums or arts centres mean to the people who use them. And how people can be brought together when culture is used as a catalyst.

More importantly, perhaps, OPEN asks how they can respond to their own reality. China is so socially, economically, and politically different from Europe and North America and, in many cases, these centres for culture do not contain a formal collection, nor are they planned or conceived with a specific cultural remit in mind, which is the definition of an international model for a cultural space. So, does this model translate well? Should a museum reflect its own regional influences? Certainly, elements of the Western museum model translate to China, but, unencumbered by history, these cultural buildings have wider possibilities. How, then, can they be made a part of the city and valued by the local community?

Li Hu and Wenjing are partners in life as well as architecture. Their very personal and professional dynamic is driven by the combination of his animated energy and her quiet, thoughtful personality. More often than not, architects work in isolation or within a traditional office hierarchy, but at their Beijing studio, Li Hu and Wenjing constantly challenge each other's creative ideas until there is a convergence of minds.

Their creative and intellectual influences and interests are many and varied. Both read voraciously and look to nature for inspiration, collecting objects such as shells and stones, and they have always been interested in art and culture. Until the COVID-19 pandemic halted international movement, they travelled widely, visiting Europe and the United States, and South America. It was in South America that they became particularly interested in the radical designs of Italian-Brazilian architect Lina Bo Bardi, and especially in her commitment to an inclusive societal environment. Le Corbusier remains an important influence—particularly his Le Couvent de La Tourette in France and his concept of *promenade architecturale*, according to which the layout of a building naturally creates a sense of continuity, inviting movement from one space to the next—as does the American architect Louis Kahn. Musicians such as John Lennon; artists such as Van Gogh; and philosophers Laozi, Zhuangzi, and Socrates have also contributed toward shaping the ideas and spirit of OPEN.

Perhaps their most important design concept is the way they constantly strive to create spaces that are welcoming and engaging, and where people want to meet. Li Hu and Wenjing are not alone in thinking about equality in terms of cultural access, and China today provides an ideal, largely unconstrained, environment in which to experiment with finding a delicate balance between surprise, modernisation, and usefulness, and to put nature and people first. They appreciate that they are working at a particularly exciting time, when things can change in consequential ways.

Huang Wenjing (left), Li Hu (right);
and OPEN's studio, Beijing (below
and bottom)

Community is very diverse in China, and Li Hu and Wenjing take particular care to understand whom they work for. This is especially the case when it comes to digital convergence and the need for cultural institutions to be audience-focused and relevant. In closing museums, libraries, and performing arts centres around the world, COVID-19 has made us realise the importance of these pillars in our lives, and that we need to use digital tools more effectively.

Of course these are important questions for all cultural institutions, but architects have a special responsibility to think about how a building and its landscape can extend to be part of the social fabric; to engage in novel ways with wider, larger audiences; and to meet—or to set—higher expectations. OPEN's approach to designing a cultural space with a new form and energy, which will become a social platform for the community, is so sensible and sensitive that one would expect such an approach to be used just about everywhere, and by more architects. It is not. Although there is precedent for the potential to reshape our cultural experience, albeit in vastly different contexts, Lina Bo Bardi's SESC Pompéia, for example, and Renzo Piano and Richard Rogers's Centre Pompidou have shown what can be achieved when architecture is bold and playful, and when it brings a different perspective.

Perhaps this is when Li Hu and Wenjing's insider-outsider status stands them in good stead. Their architectural training outside China means that they draw on the whole world, while their life in China enables them to navigate the cultural and bureaucratic challenges, and to adapt quickly. There is no roadmap to follow in China, but, given our current moment, the social concerns of architecture, and the urgency of sustainability and environmentalism, they believe that they stand on the cusp of something new and important: their primary responsibility as Chinese architects is how they might contribute to a more sustainable future for architecture by helping others to look at cultural buildings in a different way. In doing so, they show the power of architecture that is built not just around utility and form, but also around the experience of culture.

Indeed, OPEN is the perfect name for an architectural design studio that is determined to bring a new spirit to the reimagining of tradition by creating meaningful, fluid cultural spaces that welcome and engage everyone, and that ask a visitor to experience the site as a whole environment.

CONVERSATION

A conversation between Martino
Stierli, the Philip Johnson Chief
Curator of Architecture and Design at
The Museum of Modern Art (MoMA),
New York, and Huang Wenjing and Li Hu,
architects and cofounders of OPEN.

Moderator: Catherine Shaw

June 30, 2021

CATHERINE: Martino, the Chinese know a lot about what is happening around the world in terms of architecture and design, but who is interested in what is happening in China?

MARTINO: A young generation of Chinese architects are very well educated and cosmopolitan, and truly interested in what is going on elsewhere. Conversely, in the West, knowledge of what is happening in contemporary China is rather limited and distorted to some degree. I think it has to do with long-standing perceptions and orientalist reflexes. When I visited China for the first time, about five years ago, I had an image in my mind that it would be a place where mainly Western 'starchitects' built gigantic, spectacular buildings that are, for the most part, contextless—beautiful architectural sculptures that don't really relate to the specific cultural environment. I was very excited to find a younger generation of local architects interested in defining an architecture that is more rooted in and responsive to the specific cultural context.

WENJING: We came back to China because Li Hu was representing one of those starchitect offices at the time,[1] but now I feel we are at another stage, and a new generation of Chinese architects is building meaningfully and substantially. However, I am curious about how you noticed our work in the sea of Chinese architects. What do you see in us?

MARTINO: Li Xiangning[2] first introduced us in Beijing on my first visit there several years ago. He introduced me to a lot of your peers, and some of them I found more interesting, and some less so—you were among those whom I was curious about. I also had a chance to visit Tank Shanghai (see pp.60–97) and UCCA Dune (see pp.24–59) in person, both of which are interesting contributions as cultural institutions that go beyond a conventional understanding of certain typologies.

I'm particularly interested in questions of 'adaptive reuse,'[3] not only for ecological concerns, but also for what I call cultural sustainability. The massive urbanisation and transformation of Chinese society in the past three decades has left many disoriented and longing for a sense of place and belonging. The industrial revolution of the second half of the twentieth century is very much part of Chinese history now, and a project like Tank Shanghai is a relevant way to reference this history, while also updating that legacy with a new use. I find it a very interesting and meaningful proposition: it is a project that opens up a former site of industrial infrastructure to the public by means of a generous park with a variety of cultural offerings. Likewise, UCCA Dune provides cultural offerings in a rapidly developing coastal community, while at the same time sensitively interacting with the natural environment and protecting the dune landscape. While it is not one of those spectacular structures that vie for your attention, its cavernous spaces create a very memorable image. The experiential dimension of walking through it is about how these interior spaces are intrinsically linked to the natural environment. Of course, it is artificial, but it gives you the feeling of being part of the natural environment, which I find extraordinary.

WENJING: It is important to us that the architecture helped to define a new kind of institution at the Tank Shanghai project. We refer to it as the 'museum without boundaries' and brought the park in both as a requirement and an instrument. I often use the analogy of Central Park, in New York, for how a cultural institution can be an equaliser. Everybody can use and enjoy the park, and it is open and generous. For us, in Shanghai, the park tries to bring more people to or near the art institution, so the institution doesn't just cater to the privileged few, but also to anyone enjoying a picnic who may then glimpse the art and wander in. I see that as the opposite to The Met, which sits with its back to Central Park, with solid walls and dumpsters separating the two. We are lucky to be in an environment receptive to innovation. Tank Shanghai is a new institution—it didn't exist before—so in many ways it follows the form and vision of its architecture, and will evolve into a new, much more inclusive, and open kind of art centre.

MARTINO: That is an interesting point. In the West, cultural institutions are thinking hard about the democratisation of space, and of giving access to people who would not normally go to cultural amenities and institutions, and I think that is really commendable and is, in fact, essential. Cultural institutions such as museums are often perceived as elitist. The experiential side of architecture as part of the visual-spatial experience is very strong in your architectural thinking. Through it, architecture becomes part of everyday life: a suggestion that people engage, as opposed to just providing them with a service. In a way, it is giving agency to people to make use of the space in a way that they like, and in ways that are not necessarily scripted by the architects.

There is something that I am curious to hear your thoughts on: An enormous number of cultural centres and institutions have been built in China over the years, and the sense that I get, coming from the West, is that many of these places are empty and essentially unprogrammed. It is not clearly defined from the outset what function they are going to serve. Conversely, in the West, when you undertake such a big, expensive project, you have a very specific idea of what the building will be used for—an opera house, a performance centre—but at Tank Shanghai, it's almost as if the architectural imagination sets the table for what the programme will be.

LI HU: Martino, you have indeed noticed something unique in the phenomenon that some buildings are being built without content—or even a clear purpose in extreme cases.

MARTINO: Do you think that China is a latecomer to the 'Bilbao effect,' as many have argued?[4] In other words, do you think the Chinese are using contemporary architecture as a brand to attract new investment with the ultimate objective of transforming and gentrifying entire neighbourhoods?

LI HU: It would take decades to do things the same way as in the West, where you have an art group or foundation, and then you plan a space for it. Inevitably, in China, there will be voids or emptiness to be filled. During the COVID-19 pandemic, I have noticed how, because there are so few domestic performances, opera houses and theatres in China have ended up showing videos. Tank Shanghai is having problems engaging performers from outside China, but because of the way it integrates with the landscape, and because the interior is flexible and adaptable, they are able to bring in many different things instead, like fashion shows and performances, and big events by international names like Louis Vuitton.

What interests me particularly in this situation are, as you mentioned, the opportunities for architecture, and how we can contribute to the discourse. What is urgent? What is relevant? I think it is important to listen to the faint but urgent voices calling for change. That agenda is not unique to China, but what is unique here is that we are not well connected to our past, and we have been going through rapid changes technologically, socially, and economically. So, in many ways, the country is starting new cultural traditions.

MARTINO: I see that as a challenge, but also an opportunity.

CATHERINE: Martino, do you think now is a good time for a radical rethink of cultural institutions, their role in society, and their design?

MARTINO: I think this is a good time to reflect on what cultural institutions have been historically, and what we want them to be going forward. It is no longer sufficient if cultural institutions such as museums or theatres see themselves as temples of the muses. Rather, they aspire to be places of conversation and social interaction. I think the work of OPEN and some of their colleagues is going in that direction. This is one of the reasons why MoMA acquired a substantial body of works from contemporary Chinese architects last year, the work of OPEN included. One aspect that many of these projects share and that is relevant to me is the idea of creating spaces for new commonalities—in other words,

that there is a strong investment in civic space. While it is problematic that many such buildings are built and then remain unused, Tank Shanghai is a good example where this works well. It provides a public park and a restaurant, and a free space for people to do things that they couldn't do elsewhere in a very densely populated city like Shanghai. I think these kinds of shared common spaces are deeply meaningful for a society such as the Chinese that has undergone such radical and, at times, traumatic transformations in the more recent past.

A second aspect of contemporary Chinese architecture that I find noteworthy—and it's related to the first proposition—is a realisation in China that this hyper-urbanisation has come to an impasse, and it is necessary to rethink all the rural areas that have been depopulated and left behind, and to use architecture to reinvigorate local economies and provide livelihoods outside the urban megacentres. I believe this realisation has the power to serve as a model for many other places in the world, including the US, where we have become painfully aware of the increasing gap between the affluent urban elite and people in post-industrial cities or rural parts of the country, who feel left behind and disengaged with contemporary culture. That produces a lot of political division, and I believe this kind of rethinking about what happens outside the cities is very urgent, and not only in China.

The third aspect for me is the question of ecology. We are at a breaking point globally where we have to find a different way to deal with our limited resources. We have to develop an architecture that is less extractive and more sustainable culturally, ecologically, and economically. Over the past three decades, China has become the largest construction site in history, and we have now come to a point where we realise that it cannot go on like this forever. So, projects like Tank Shanghai give me hope, because it does not pursue a tabula rasa approach, but looks first at what is already there and how it can be reused in an imaginative and inventive way. This kind of reuse not only provides a feeling of place and history in the sense of cultural sustainability, it is, at the same time, ecologically conscious.

WENJING: I want to go back to your observation about all the civic architecture that is being built. There is a general feeling that China has developed very fast and needs to catch up on culture, so there is a strong push from the top down for cultural buildings. It is easier to build something than to fill it with meaningful content, as we said, but I can see a younger generation who are growing up interested in art and the theatre, and so things will start to change. It is true that we often receive commissions without knowing who the operator will be—at Tank Shanghai, for example, we only got to know the operator halfway through the building process. The push is to build something quickly, and if we were cynics, we could just create beautiful objects, because there is no one scrutinising what we do from the user's perspective. But we have our own agenda and values, and we want to bring those into our buildings and to use this opportunity to shape buildings flexibly for the future. We also have to be extremely self-disciplined, which includes making sure our buildings work well and maximise the impact of the resources that are invested.

LI HU: We need more civic buildings. The Bilbao effect has happened across China, but when you are asked to build a civic landmark, you can create one that is beautiful and you can also build one that works. We don't just play the role of architect, but often help the client to imagine the result too. We were not asked for a cultural building at our Sun Tower (see pp.190–209) landmark—the client wanted something symbolic like the Vessel[5] in New York—but we convinced them that such an undertaking needs to be more than a sculpture, and we made it easy to operate and maintain too. So many institutions are badly run or empty and, obviously, very few institutions have the capacity of MoMA, so when you don't have the resources, what do you do? How do you make a museum without a foundation? A library that is also a concert hall and café? What I find exciting

about working in China is that, despite the difficulties, we can create something that is more than architecture.

CATHERINE: If the context and the way cultural architecture is designed and used is so radically different in China, then what are the similarities with the avant-garde cultural architecture that you see elsewhere?

MARTINO: The segment of contemporary Chinese architecture I am interested in references certain cultural and material contexts, and it is very much part of a global conversation about what contemporary cultural architecture is. I think the concept of a museum in China is quite different from the Western understanding, where it has traditionally been defined as a place that collects artistic objects and preserves them in perpetuity. In China, museums often don't have collections so, from the Western perspective, by definition, they are not museums, they are really multi-functional exhibition spaces. It is interesting to observe that there is quite obviously the political will to provide such buildings. The government apparently feels that large swathes of the population have not had access to high culture, so now they want to provide culture like opera, but although China has its own very long history of opera, theatres have primarily been built according to Western artistic conventions. In the West, these conventions emerged out of local traditions and became stablised over many centuries, and the danger is that these buildings may become totally unanchored and irrelevant to what local people want or care about. So, I think that what OPEN is doing is to subvert this in a very productive way, and to open up institutions without a programme, providing people with a cultural space that potentially means something to them and they can identify with. I believe this notion of agency—the agency of the users—is seminal for the success of a new cultural institution.

I believe it is important to understand that a culture is not just something we consume, that we watch, and that has nothing to do with us. Culture is very much an expression and an investigation of our values and how we inhabit the world collectively, and how we aspire to live. If cultural institutions succeed in providing spaces for citizens to collectively ask and reflect on these questions—the park at Tank Shanghai, for example, or the smaller theatre in the Pingshan Performing Arts Centre (see pp.98–127)—that is precisely what makes these buildings meaningful and not just alien objects that don't connect to people's lives.

LI HU: Increasingly, there is conflict between imported and local things, and soon there will be a trend towards more adaptive, informal, and flexible projects. I especially admire the work of Lina Bo Bardi,[6] who moved away from São Paulo and worked with local groups in native settlements. She designed and also worked with them in art and dance, and music, creating something grounded in the local.

MARTINO: I am also a great fan of Lina Bo Bardi. Her SESC Pompéia, the adaptive reuse and transformation of a former drum factory into a cultural centre in São Paulo,[7] is one of my favourite buildings anywhere in the world and, in a way, you could say Tank Shanghai is not dissimilar, because you also have this former industrial complex and are trying to create a cultural institution that benefits the local population.

LI HU: We visited Brazil two years ago and, when we entered the SESC Pompéia Factory, we found that people were relaxed, which was quite like what we see at Tank Shanghai. I think it is important for people to be themselves and want to be part of it all. You could see a lot of different types of people and that is the ideal. That is the future of the world.

MARTINO: I think that is the future that architecture can give to the world. It is this kind of project that gives me hope.

CATHERINE: What about established organisations like MoMA? How challenging is it for you to adapt? You're seeing this architectural experience elsewhere—what can you take for yourself? Or is it too different?

MARTINO: I think it is very different, but there is an urgency for MoMA in the current cultural situation, and in coming out of the experience of the pandemic. MoMA has always been able to rely on a steady stream of international and domestic tourists coming to the museum. Then, suddenly, that was gone, which really has been an eye-opener for us as an institution—we want to be more than just a stop on the tourist circuit for people who come to New York for four days to check MoMA off their list. We want to be a citizen of New York and engaged with the issues and problems, and interests of our local community. We want to make the people of New York feel that MoMA is a place for them as much as it is a place for overseas visitors. MoMA has often been perceived as an elitist institution that speaks to the cultural jet set but has no bearing on everyday people. But I think the pandemic has given new urgency to our commitment to not only be a place where the world meets, but also one where New Yorkers feel at home. I believe the recent expansion by Diller Scofidio + Renfro, which opened in the fall of 2019, just half a year before the lockdown, was a significant architectural step in this direction—for example, by making the ground floor free and accessible to anyone, even without a ticket.

But, beyond that, there is a lot of curatorial work to be done. We are trying to reimagine the institution, to make it more open and participatory, where people engage and interact. American society and New York is increasingly a multicultural, multiethnic society, and if you don't, as a cultural institution, engage with such social transformations, you become a dinosaur and die—you become irrelevant.

CATHERINE: The way younger people interact, from shopping to working, and how they live, is changing and it seems to be trickling into the cultural sector. In China, we see changes happening within a year or two, which completely transform the landscape. For cultural organisations worldwide that must be a concern?

MARTINO: Yes, although I do not believe in the theory that the digital will supersede the analogue. I think the digital will complement it. I think if the long months of the lockdown and the social isolation have taught us something, it is an awareness that we long for and, indeed, depend on . . . I hate the word 'authentic,' but what I mean is the physical experience of being in a real space with real objects and in company with real people. In this sense, I think the digital is not a threat to cultural institutions; it is a huge opportunity to bring awareness to what we have to offer digital natives—young people who have never been to a museum—and to draw them in by a number of new digital tools. Once you have been to a museum, you understand that an image on your iPhone is completely different from standing in front of a real painting, with its haptic dimension and its quality as an object.

CATHERINE: **It makes all the difference when you are actually at an exhibition and can experience the translation from architecture to model in person, as most exhibitions of architecture show models.**

MARTINO: Exactly.

WENJING: I think social media and the internet help to demystify a lot of things. Nowadays, before people visit a place, say a museum, they will have, most likely, already googled the place, the exhibition, and the artists. They have more information. On the other hand, when people read about a painting on their smartphone, they often want to see it in real life, to see how it truly looks. What I have learned from Tank Shanghai is how much the definition of art and culture has expanded, even in places traditionally related to commerce, and how technologies can also be an integral part of art exhibitions. Nowadays, boundaries are being rapidly redefined. I very much agree with Martino that China has imported the concept of cultural institutions from the West, and this is both our problem and our opportunity. It is about time that something new is invented which is both connected to the world and to our past and future.

LI HU: What Martino mentioned about changes at MoMA are also taking place in many other established institutions. Globally, I see more similarities than differences, and collaboration and exchange are becoming more important because humanity is sharing similar urgencies. In China, if we can understand the need for change, there will be an opportunity for something new.

WENJING: I don't think the Western media see the level of detail and thinking and passion; there are plenty of beautiful objects coming from Chinese architects, and a lot of this plays into the Western notion of what Chinese orientalism ought to be. I feel a lot of the opportunities to do something different are overlooked—and are hard to recognise from images alone.

LI HU: That is the challenge for Martino curating architecture. Unlike art, architecture exhibitions can't show the real thing, so there are just the model and photographs. You can't show the most important things—the impact and experience.

MARTINO: That is the perennial dilemma of architectural exhibitions, but, even so, there are engaging ways to show how spaces are being used, from cinematic *promenades architecturales* to the new possibilities of virtual and enhanced reality, which will likely change the ways in which architecture is exhibited. It is true that Instagram and our image-driven digital culture have the tendency and run the risk of reducing complex spatial phenomena to superficial, photogenic representations. For this reason, it is not enough for an architectural exhibition to just show pretty photographs—you can look at those on your own screen. Instead, we often opt for a multimedia presentation that includes not just photographs, but also sketches, drawings, models, and so on. This allows curators to convey a sense of complexity and depth, but also of materiality and experience.

CATHERINE: What is your upcoming exhibition about and why should the audience engage with it?

MARTINO: The first exhibition, *Renew, Reuse, Recycle: Recent Architecture from China*, is a thematic exhibition, and draws exclusively on contemporary Chinese architecture, but we believe the topic addressed here is relevant to contemporary architecture anywhere, for the reasons outlined earlier. The exhibition contends that contemporary Chinese architecture is a model case to study what should be happening with regard to environmental and cultural sustainabilty. In addition, I hope the exhibition will rectify misconceptions of what contemporary Chinese architecture is, which I think are still very much anchored to this notion of mega projects by starchitects from ten to fifteen years ago.

WENJING: I know that adaptive reuse has been much discussed in the US and UK. Is that why you are using this term for the exhibition? Was it a way to bring China into this global conversation?

MARTINO: Not all the projects we are including in the exhibition are about adaptive reuse. Some are about cultural sustainability and engaging with local craft traditions and material culture. For example, I think of your Chapel of Sound (see pp.158–189): it is a new building and, even though it is not in the exhibition, it would be a good fit because it is in rural China and particularly references a natural context, geology, and experimentation, which I find a very productive approach for culture generally.

CATHERINE: Having not been able to travel to China for the past two years during the COVID-19 pandemic, what are the questions in the forefront of your mind about contemporary cultural architecture in China?

MARTINO: There are two questions. The first one concerns the role of the architect. I don't think people understand how differently an architectural office operates in China.

The other question is about the famous speech by Chinese President Xi Jinping[8] that called for an end to the 'weird architecture' from China's boom period. I don't think the West really understands what that means, and I'd be interested to hear if it has had a direct effect on your work, or if it has made a difference to the Chinese architectural culture in the last five years or so?

LI HU: First, I think that the most interesting part of being an architect is having to play multiple roles—more than you can imagine. You have to be a planner and an architect, but you also have to be a researcher and engineer and scientist, and a strategist too. And you have to be almost a politician to get the work through—and an experienced contractor to have it properly built. And, most importantly, you have to dream things up from nowhere, rather than any inherited, specific type of thing.

Secondly, since the president's speech, I, personally, have continued to see weird architecture going up. I think different people understand what weird architecture means differently. There is now an annual list of the ten ugliest buildings in China, published by a group of critics and scholars, which is stirring up a lot of debate over what is ugly. Of the ten ugliest buildings, some are really ugly, and some are weird, and some works by foreign architects are on the list. But what really strikes me is emptiness. You spend a huge amount of money on building something completely useless—to me, *that* is ugly. It is an interesting debate about value judgement.

MARTINO: Of course language and its meaning are a cultural construction, and what is weird to you may not be weird to me.

LI HU: This is a chaotic time for value systems around the world. If you look at the recent ten most important cultural facilities architectural competition in Shenzhen[9]—that is the biggest deal in China. Over the past eighteen months, the competition for tabula rasa cultural buildings—an opera house, museums, and big universities—has caused a heated debate.

WENJING: And most of the ten finalists are by foreign starchitects.

MARTINO: That seems to reaffirm the old paradigm—that is interesting, and a bit disappointing.

WENJING: The selection represents forces that still bow to foreign status and star power, although there is more discussion going on now and voices on the internet debating against this selection process, which recognises the design power that has developed internally in China.

LI HU: It is the reality, but what is interesting in China is what is happening on the margins.

MARTINO: I agree. As early as 1924, José Ortega y Gasset argued in 'The Dehumanization of Art' that artists occupying the margins of modernity are best positioned to reconfigure art's functions. And, while we may live in a very different historical moment, in our exhibition, we make a point of saying that the interesting things in China are often happening either in the secondary cities—places that no one in New York has ever heard of—or in rural areas.

CATHERINE: Are those not where architects have the best opportunity to express their creative vision and values? Where they have more freedom to create the architecture that they aspire to?

LI HU: Yes, but I hope public resources will be spent more wisely for the public good, like what I saw by Lina Bo Bardi in São Paulo. Those were major public buildings, and I do hope that we will get on the right track, sooner rather than later.

WENJING: Another point to make is that a younger generation of Chinese architects is resorting to less-organised areas. We see a lot of Airbnb projects in rural areas, for example, that are not strictly regulated by building codes and official reviews, so they can be more free. The countryside in China is very different to the West—it is a whole other big topic. Working on complicated public projects in a city makes your life much harder, but I guess we chose this difficult route.

LI HU: I think Wenjing's point is to not retreat from the battleground or challenge. That is what is special about OPEN—we have not retreated to the countryside—we want to be in the urban centres and to find opportunities to do things that are truly public, and not just in a comfortable niche.

WENJING: To stay in the architectural comfort zone would be to stay with disciplinary concerns, visual language, materials, the craft—which are all relatively easy to control by an architect. But the reason we chose to leave New York for the battle zone was because we want to do something meaningful, something that will have more impact. Our dilemma is that we are interested in public works and complex urban issues, and, in China, we are used to these opportunities being in the hands of state-owned design institutes or foreign starchitects. We are hoping for more real projects, like the Tank Shanghai—a rare opportunity for a small office like ours—and the Pingshan Performing Arts Centre too.

LI HU: I still think we are working on the margins, but perhaps a better phrase is working in the cracks in the system, where you may find some freedom.

MARTINO: I think that is a very useful metaphor. The concept of the margin perhaps tends to reaffirm obsolete hierarchies between centre and (so-called) periphery, when so many relevant things are happening outside of the hegemonic centres of discourse. I like the metaphor of the crack because it helps audiences who are not familiar with the subject matter to understand that China is not just one homogeneous space that is governed and totally controlled by a singular doctrine, but that it produces gaps that can be exploited for artistic and architectural experimentation, and for civic discourse.

LI HU: To end on a promising note, in recent years, we have started to see younger clients in both the public and private sectors. I just met a young local politician in a new district, and he was so energetic and wants to do something exciting, which I think is very promising. In China, you can probably see this young generation emerging more than anywhere else.

MARTINO: If they get traction on a wider scale—and let's hope they do—it will be very exciting.

1　Steven Holl Architects, New York, United States.

2　Li Xiangning is full professor and dean at Tongji University College of Architecture and Urban Planning, Shanghai.

3　Adaptive reuse refers to the repurposing of an existing structure for new use. For example, converting a historic train station into a hotel.

4　The Bilbao effect refers to the leap in tourist numbers in the ex-industrial Spanish town following the opening of Frank Gehry's iconic Guggenheim Bilbao Museum.

5　A fifteen-storey, open-air structure, designed by Thomas Heatherwick, with a honeycomb-like layout of staircases and landings, and clad in copper-coloured steel.

6　The architect Lina Bo Bardi (1914–1992) was Italian-born and trained, and moved to Brazil in 1946, where she produced work that reflected the country's rich cultural influences.

7　Bo Bardi's SESC Pompéia is a vast concrete cultural and community centre inserted into an old factory complex. It marked a radical departure from traditional museum design by transforming the factory into a civic space with a gallery, theatre, swimming pool, and basketball court, as well as a sun-deck and library.

8　In 2014, in a speech at a literary symposium in Beijing, President Xi Jinping expressed his distaste for unusually shaped architecture and asked that the country put a stop to 'weird' architecture.

9　In 2018, the city of Shenzhen announced plans to build ten new landmark cultural facilities—including five museums. The design competition—The Shenzhen Ten Cultural Facilities of New Era—attracted the attention of many international architects.

UCCA DUNE ART MUSEUM

Carved into an undulating dune along a serene beach near Changli in Qinhuangdao, northeast of Beijing, this contemporary art museum puts nature centre stage as it disappears into the landscape.

The single storey, 930-square-metre building was originally planned as an art space with dining functions for the Aranya community—a collection of vacation residences developed by Aranya, the forward-thinking Chinese developer. The word 'aranya' is Sanskrit for a serene location, far from human bustle, and the project that fits this definition is part of the vision of its cofounder, Ma Yin, to integrate cultural and artistic activities in residential and resort communities.

As the project progressed, Aranya entered into a strategic partnership with the UCCA Center for Contemporary Art in Beijing. Meanwhile, unconcerned with traditional ideas of what a museum should be or with making a dramatic architectural statement, the architects focused on exploring new possibilities for what an art institution can be today, looking to the natural landscape for inspiration.

"We didn't want a conventional art museum. We believe that it is important to be radical in our thinking, and to question whether traditional ideas are still valid in our new conditions, such as what modern cultural institutions should look like today, and in the future."

The architects continue, "clients often come to us looking for something different, but while drama and surprise are part of what we do, they are not everything, and nor are they the starting point of our work."

A bird's-eye view of the building (opening page); sketches by Li Hu (opposite).

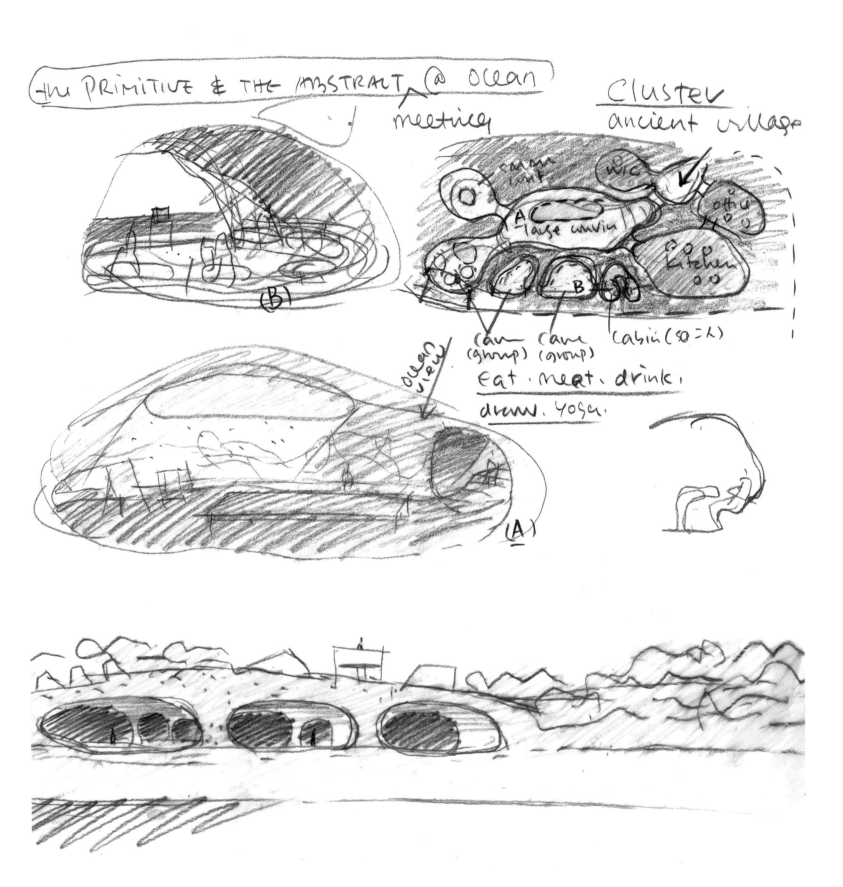

the PRIMITIVE & THE ABSTRACT @ ocean
meeting

CIuster
ancient village

(B)

(A)

ocean view

large cuuvin
A
wic
office
kitchen
cave group
B
cave (group) cave (group)
cabin (80=人)
Eat. meat. drink. draw. yoga.

THE SITE

The Bohai Sea's Gold Coast, where the Aranya community is located, is known for its sandy beaches, and the UCCA Dune Art Museum is located on an untouched stretch of beach between the ocean and land that is yet to be developed for the resort.

Dunes are rare in northern China, because there are few locations with the natural conditions that allow them to form. Until recently, there were no laws to preserve them, so many disappeared as developers decided that they blocked the sea view, which reduced a site's value.

Intrigued by the idea of creating small-scale, interesting structures that would seamlessly merge architecture, art, and nature, the architects investigated the condition of the sand dunes along the three-kilometre-long beach. They found a small section that had already suffered some damage from an unknown cause and, because of this, it was selected as the building site, as further excavation and harm to the environment would be minimised.

Li Hu and Wenjing's instinctive inclination was to create 'something primal' that would disappear into the sand:

"The paradox is that the act of building ultimately protects the dune, and the museum elevates the surrounding natural landscape to the level of art, blurring traditional boundaries between building and landscape, and between art and nature."

A happy donkey rests on the sand dune during Li Hu's first visit to the site (right); the site plan (opposite); the skylights (overleaf).

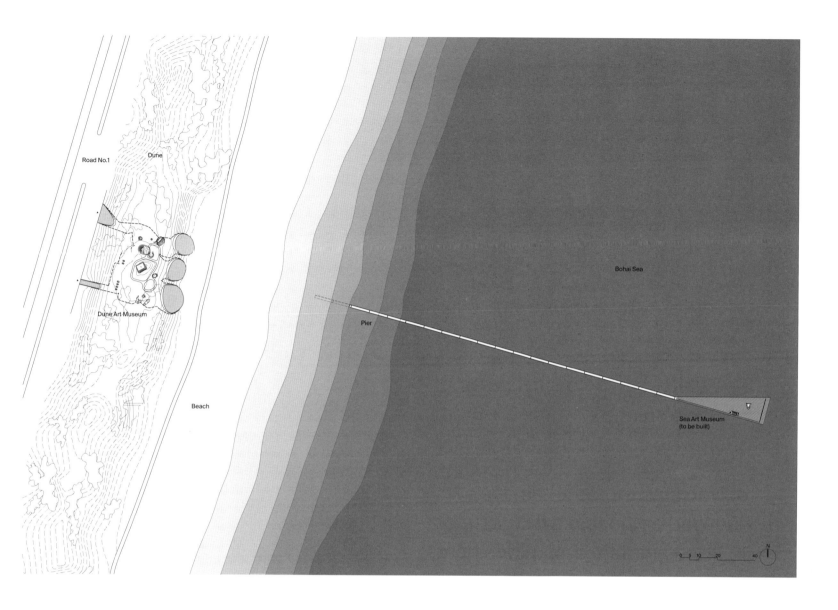

Taking the site, including the sand and ocean, as a whole ecosystem, the architects formulated a design concept with one structure inside the dune and another out to sea, creating a context to lead visitors to a dedicated gallery that will, upon completion, exhibit a single work of art at any given time.

"We see architecture as a device to establish a discourse between man and nature, framing and building a context, and an emotional connection."

The effect is one of pilgrimage, as the walkway linking the UCCA Dune Art Museum to the ocean gallery will be submerged, and only visible at low tide, emphasising the contrast between solitude and community, organic shapes and crisp geometry.

"It is a very different way of looking at the built environment," Li Hu says, "one that values disappearing and blending into nature."

Once the crucial decision was made to build inside the dune rather than, as traditionally, over it, the building's fluid silhouette developed very quickly. Structural and architectural modelling helped to shape optimal contours that would reflect the dune's gentle, natural outline, formlessness, and unpredictability, while holding back the pressure of the surrounding sand.

The basic form also attests to the architects' research into ancient settlements where, typically, a large space had smaller clusters around it, which created a protective sanctuary. For Li Hu, this fitted naturally into the dune's long history, and with the earliest recorded discoveries of art and civilisation in caves.

For Li Hu and Wenjing, it is essential for designers to understand the origins of culture, yet also feel the freedom to question which sources are still valid, particularly in China, where contemporary society is still developing, and cultural institutions are reinventing themselves.

"We feel there is still the chance to do things differently in China, and not be pressured by cultural norms from other milieus, which may not translate into our situation," Li Hu explains.

The hidden quality also corresponded to the architects' interpretation of traditional Chinese landscape paintings, where pavilions and villages are not usually shown as distinct objects.

The reality of development in China is that architects don't always control the frame of reference, and they must be flexible. For example, they must be ready to act when an interesting opportunity presents itself, such as transforming Ma's idea for mixing dining with art into a design for a museum that is dedicated solely to art. OPEN recalls:

> Ma immediately understood that making the building into an art installation dedicated to nature would fulfil deeper emotional and spiritual needs, and UCCA's curators were willing to tailor their exhibitions to fit the museum's extraordinary solitary setting. We were very excited, even though the design was already under construction when Ma and UCCA went into partnership, and went back to the drawing board to redesign a substantial part of the building to accommodate an art museum.

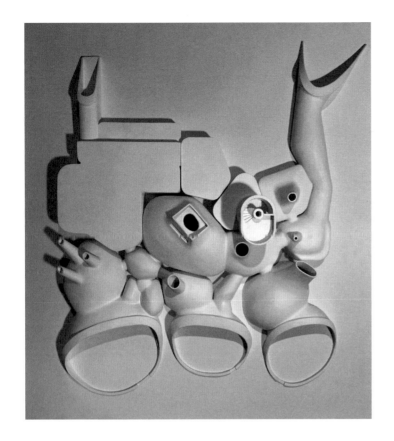

A physical model of the building.

Ground-floor Plan

1. Main entrance
2. Lobby
3. Gallery
4. Café
5. Stairs
6. Outdoor exhibition terrace
7. Toilet
8. Secondary entrance
9. Service entrance
10. Geothermal plant
11. Power distribution room
12. Electrical room
13. Spare room

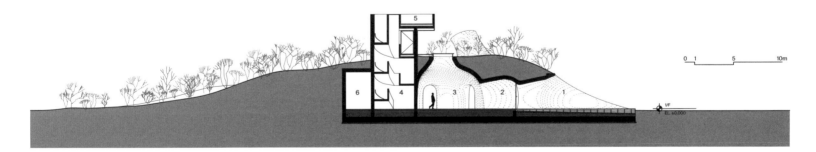

Section AA

1. Outdoor exhibition terrace
2. Secondary entrance
3. Gallery
4. Stairs
5. Viewing platform
6. Toilet

Gallery Skylight

Direct sunlight from 18 April to 15 August;
No direct sunlight on the display wall

Annual sun path for gallery skylight
Direct sunlight from 4 February to 15 August

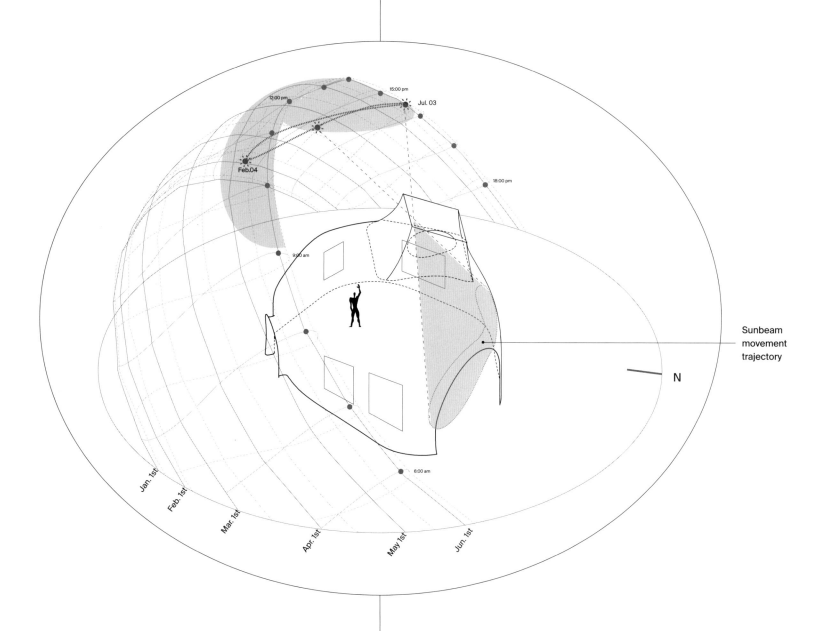

Sunbeam
movement
trajectory

N

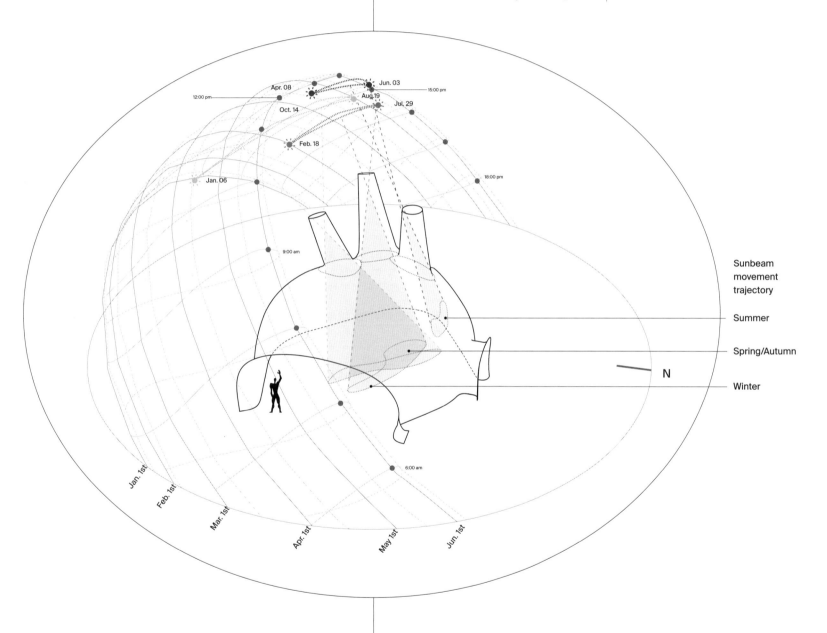

Gallery skylights

Direct sunlight throughout the year

Annual sunpath for spring/autumn skylight;
Direct sunlight from 1 January to 1 May and from 18 August to 31 December

Annual sun path for winter skylight:
Direct sunlight from 18 February to 14 October

Annual sun path for summer skylight:
Direct sunlight from 8 April to 2 September

Jun. 03

Apr. 08

12:00 pm

Aug.19

15:00 pm

Oct. 14

Jul. 29

Feb. 18

Jan. 06

18:00 pm

9:00 am

Sunbeam
movement
trajectory

Summer

Spring/Autumn

N

Winter

6:00 am

Jan. 1st

Feb. 1st

Mar. 1st

Apr. 1st

May 1st

Jun. 1st

The main entrance and lobby (above); three skylights, with different orientations, in a smaller gallery (right); a beam of daylight from the large skylight above (opposite).

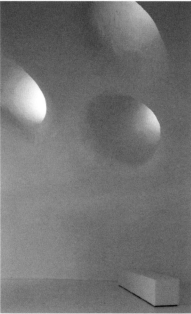

The original plan for a dining room had allocated space for a large kitchen and a very special public bathroom, which were no longer needed. So both became exhibition spaces, and several smaller, yet still distinctive, bathrooms were carved out. The designs for the skylights were changed to light up paintings and sculptures.

Each room in the museum is unrepeated and unrepeatable, and, therefore, they have different requirements. For example, the main, central room has a large double-layered skylight that, from the ground, appears to be a simple circular opening to the sky. However, above this opening there is an upper layer composed of a giant rectangular skylight with a horizontal shading device that is completely out of sight. The complicated geometry allows OPEN to harness the trajectory of sunlight as it appears at different times of the day and year onto the floor, instead of the walls, and infuse every radius of the space with a monastic ambience.

The soft curves connect with its context in the dune and the matte, rustic interior walls diffuse and modulate natural sunlight, creating pools of light that vary in intensity and help orientate visitors within the dramatic internal landscape. The architects see lighting and materials as inseparably linked, and, as one of the most important ways to associate with nature, these two fundamental elements help visitors to slow down to observe, and feel, the passing of time, and to identify profoundly with the cosmos.

"For us, nature is everything, not just plants, so the movement of the sun and the changing colours and textures on the wall during the day are very important considerations."

"We never start designing with a particular image in mind. Instead, we think about the sensation of moving through the building because that means we consider the different materialities and drama, and how they make you feel."

Li Hu and Wenjing are both particularly intrigued by the interaction between water and sand. They have taken the effect of this interaction and created an ever-changing texture throughout the museum. Drawing further inspiration from the materials on their very doorstep, broken seashells that have been in the sea for a long time fascinate them too:

Ancient Taoism follows the flow of nature instead of competing with it. A humble symbiotic relationship with the natural environment is of benefit to everyone, and we always try to view our work from this perspective.

An outdoor exhibition terrace that faces the sea.

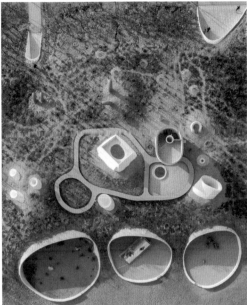

"We can sense the fragility of the ecosystem," Wenjing explains. "The ocean may appear calm, but then rapidly become violent and destroy buildings on the shore, so, instead of confronting the extreme powers of nature, we seek protection from them by hiding in the dune. Interestingly, this very action turns out to have protected the dune from being demolished by real estate development."

An aerial view of the dune (opposite); the concrete shell underneath the dune (top left); the restored sand dune completed in October 2018 (top middle); the native plant life flourishing during the summer in 2019 (top right).

The spiral staircase (top left);
the interconnected gallery spaces
(top right).

The project is not conventional architecture in terms of form or the spatial and organisational relationship of rooms.

It is not just dome-shaped, but three-dimensional, and there are no corridors because the chambers are more like living cells, squeezed together, creating a curious series of adjacencies and interactions: 'A society of rooms, each different yet equal.' Even the stairs are a cell-like space.

Light shows the way through the building. Since the main entrance is down a dark tunnel, the light at the end draws visitors along to the small lobby, then to the large skylight at the centre of the main room, and then there is oceanside light from the windows. Finally, a brighter light from above illuminates the otherwise dim staircase that spirals up to the rooftop garden, where there is an open view of the ocean and the whole horizon.

The spiral staircase (right);
Sunrise seen from the rooftop (bottom).

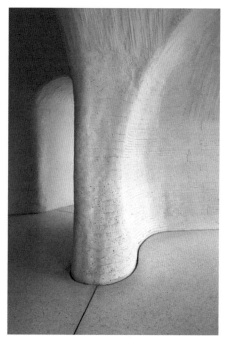

The doorways between galleries (far left, top and bottom); the concrete wall and floor (left); the main gallery (top right); a drum-shaped skylight drops down from the gallery roof (middle right); the tunnel at the main entrance (bottom right); the opening towards the sea (overleaf).

The relationship between architecture and light creates a natural pathway for visitors to move easily through the various subterranean areas, orientating themselves more naturally in the larger room in the middle. Whereas all the other rooms are autonomous, and visitors go through a kind of threshold-doorway to the next space, this main, central chamber intersects with a smaller room, representing a moment when two cells collide, "as perfect as the curve that divides them," Li Hu says.

The intuitive layout obviates the need for extensive signage. Instead, at the entrance, a clay model on the wall shows the building's simple form.

It also helps to retain the sense of surprise, which is one of the deepest delights in architecture. As the museum is small and intimate, and the intensity and direction of light guides them through the site, visitors move spontaneously and discover things.

According to Li Hu, a contextual connection does not always need to be obvious or formal in architecture, but it must feel natural and authentic.

Early plans envisaged an inch of smooth plaster on the walls, but as soon as the formwork was taken away from the concrete, the designers decided to keep the crude yet unexpectedly beautiful rustic texture. Many of the construction workers had been boatbuilders with years of experience shaping curvilinear geometries by hand, and so the outstanding artisanal quality they brought to the finish became a defining quality of the building.

However, the procedure was not without its challenges: It was an eye-opening experience that demonstrated all the joys and frustrations of working in China. The whole process was nerve-racking, but fascinating. We had 3D-printed and computer models on site, but that is not how Chinese carpenters work. Somehow, in their minds, they already knew the exact shape and used their skills to work naturally, figuring everything out as they went along.

"It's not perfect, but that is what I love," continues Li Hu. "You can feel some part of the struggle to make it."

While the architects worked with precise coordinates on computers, construction workers meticulously formed the concrete by hand with smaller strips of wood, as if they were building a ship. The workers would request the points that they needed, and how many, and the architectural team provided precise three-dimensional coordinates generated by their computer model, which were then projected on site.

The concrete surface with the formwork texture visible inside the drum-shaped skylight (right); the formwork construction (opposite); the construction process (overleaf).

"This was fortuitous because, while joints are usually predictable, here the geometry was so complicated that they couldn't follow the perfect form lines and had to rely on their intuition and skill to make that shape. We had to trust them, and the result is that the walls tell a story about the local community, and that, in turn, becomes part of the site ecology. Architecture must belong to its time and place," the architects state.

The texture on the concrete surface (preceding pages); the skylights, walkway, and viewing platform on the roof (right); the night view from the sea (bottom); the staircase to the roof (far right).

The museum is not completely enveloped by the dune, although it cannot be seen from the street, and does not compete with the striking surrounding natural terrain. Anchored in the landscape on a two-metre-deep concrete basin, the building maintains a seamless indoor-outdoor relationship with the ocean through its large windows and the sculptural quality of the rooftop skylights. The gentle connection the museum has with nature is not just reflected in its physical appearance: hiding the building underneath the dune and creating a large overhang at the glass openings significantly reduces heat gain and loss. Meanwhile, a geothermal ground-source heat pump for air-conditioning eliminates the negative impact and emissions of a typical cooling tower.

Outside, the walkway that loops in a figure of eight—a lucky number, reminiscent of the theory of perpetual movement, a continuous mathematical dance—encourages visitors to stroll around the roof.

Sometimes the designers had to improvise on site to deal with unexpected problems. The drainage around the first skylight proved difficult to manage and there was not enough depth for soil on the roof, and so new drainage pipes were added around the edges of the skylight, with gravel to hide them. Now, this area is one of the most popular places to sit and admire the ever-changing view of the ocean and sky, and it establishes an innovative connection with nature.

The staircase is the only geometric shape in the museum, and creates a clear axis, and precise relationship, with the ocean. Three terraces and six gallery windows that face the water act as extensions from the rooms into the sand, where outdoor works of art are on display. Building on sand is complicated: despite its great load-bearing capacity, surface grains are blown so fast by the wind that there is always the danger of the doors on the beachfront terraces becoming suddenly blocked by sand piling up. On the recommendation of the local contractor, the building was raised by half a metre, and low parapets were added. These low walls surround the terrace, protect the building against the elements, and double as benches—all while creating a strong spatial relationship between inside and outside.

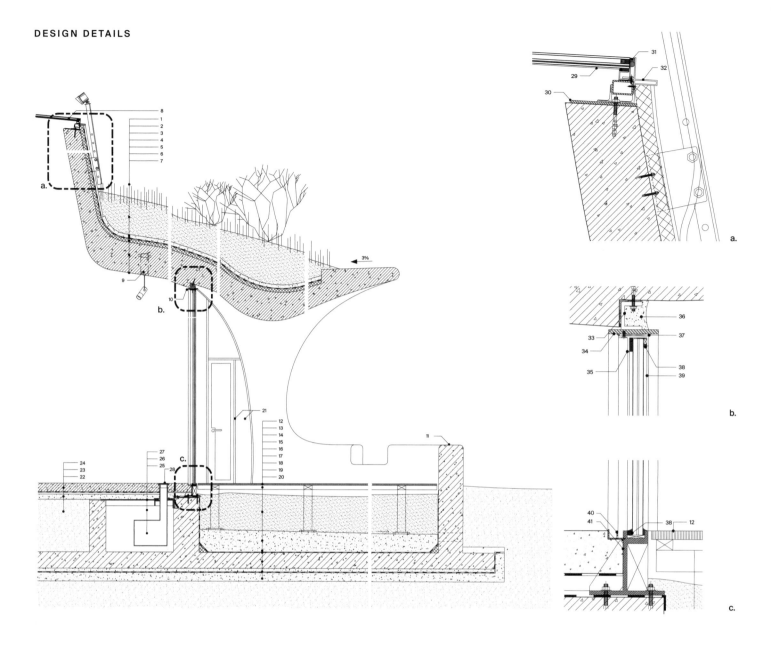

Wall section and details

1. Native dune vegetation
2. On-site sea-sand-mixed planting soil
3. 40mm C30 concrete protective layer
4. 2mm root-resistant waterproofing
5. 40mm spray-on insulation, with waterproof membrane
6. Reinforced concrete
7. White concrete protective coating
8. Skylight
9. Housing for gallery spotlight
10. Stainless-steel-framed window and door
11. Sand-blocking wall
12. Light-grey wood and plastic composite outdoor deck
13. Galvanised steel frame
14. Sand
15. C30 concrete leveling layer
16. 2mm root-resistant waterproofing
17. 1.5mm waterproof concrete coating
18. Concrete raft foundation
19. 2mm root-resistant waterproofing
20. Concrete levelling layer

21. Detachable window frame for transporting over-sized art work
22. Compacted soil
23. Concrete base layer
24. White polished concrete floor
25. Air-conditioning duct
26. Underfloor mechanical space
27. Steel plate
28. Underfloor air vent
29. Laminated insulating glass unit with low-iron glass
30. Steel plate
31. White structural silicone and sealant
32. White-painted aluminum panel
33. U-shaped stainless-steel connection piece
34. Stainless-steel curtain-wall frame, painted white
35. Stainless-steel sub-frame, painted white
36. White cement caulking
37. White sealant
38. White structural silicone and sealant
39. Laminated Insulating glass unit with low-iron glass
40. Stainless-steel channel for condensation
41. Stainless-steel curtain-wall frame, painted white

The spatial connection between all the rooms has been carefully considered and, because the entrance walkway is very small, the most convenient way to bring large works of art inside is through the oceanfront gallery-window openings, so the architects incorporated a way for one piece of window glass to be easily removed to allow large artworks to be brought inside.

Each window has a different coherent form and size. The panes of glass, made locally in Tianjin, are very large and of exceptional quality, so the room seems to expand outdoors and visitors feel they are inside the gallery but in the open air too. The organic shape of each window, and the complex construction of the surrounding concrete edge, gave the contractor the ingenious idea of taking field measurements and custom building a low-tech traditional pulley and trolley system to erect the glass, which weighs more than two tonnes.

"Twelve people moved and installed one giant pane, using only the apparatus they had designed and built themselves. It was miraculous to watch," the architects recall:

> In China, it sometimes feels like we are working chaotically, in a different universe, and improvising is a very important part of the process, so we are always deeply involved in site and construction project management.

But all these challenges are forgotten, now that the museum is open to the public as well as the Aranya community, and people are enjoying the relationship between the architecture, art, and the natural environment.

Thus, a modest building, conceived with harmony at its core, offers a novel way to unite people and culture without trying to dominate nature.

TANK SHANGHAI

How can architects create areas of belonging and inclusion? More often than not, cultural architecture generates physical thresholds and boundaries that influence access, and, in many cases, restrict how people perceive and use the spaces designed for art. In the case of Tank Shanghai, OPEN's pluralistic response to the question is typically understated, yet all the more powerful for its simplicity: they have transformed a derelict industrial site, with five aviation-fuel tanks of differing volumes, on the edge of the Huangpu River, into an attractive art centre and public park. Underneath the gently sloping, verdant landscape is a newly built structure that connects the tanks, a space that Li Hu and Wenjing call the 'Super-Surface.'

Here is a centre for art that seeks to blur the boundaries of nature, art, and architecture, and is a space for everyone.

As Li Hu explains:

> We are not very interested in creating architectural icons for cultural institutions where only a small fraction of the public— often the elite—feel a sense of belonging. Art institutions today have to evolve with society. We feel the urge to make cultural spaces more open and inclusive.

Beside the green lawns and wooden benches is a large plaza where children play in mist fountains.

The landscape on the 'Super-Surface' (opening page); a bird's-eye view of Tank Shanghai (right); the stepped waterscape (overleaf).

THE SITE

The area is part of an urban-renewal master plan to transform the Longhua district, a former industrial neighbourhood, into an eleven-kilometre waterfront cultural corridor. This endeavour has been led by the Shanghai West Bund Development Group, a state-owned development corporation, together with local government.

The nearby Shanghai DreamCenter, a mixed-use venue for cultural, entertainment, and lifestyle events, is poised to open in a transformed cement plant, and an outpost of the Centre Pompidou, the great museum of modern art in Paris, the largest in Europe, was inaugurated in 2019. As the architects recall:

> When we first saw the site it was quite stunning—definitely not something familiar to normal city life—giant, rusty oil tanks standing in a bare, open plot. The tanks each had a small, round opening in the centre of their dome, a rather striking Pantheon-like spatial quality, and sound that seems to reverberate inside forever.

Original site photos (opposite); the construction site in 2017 (below).

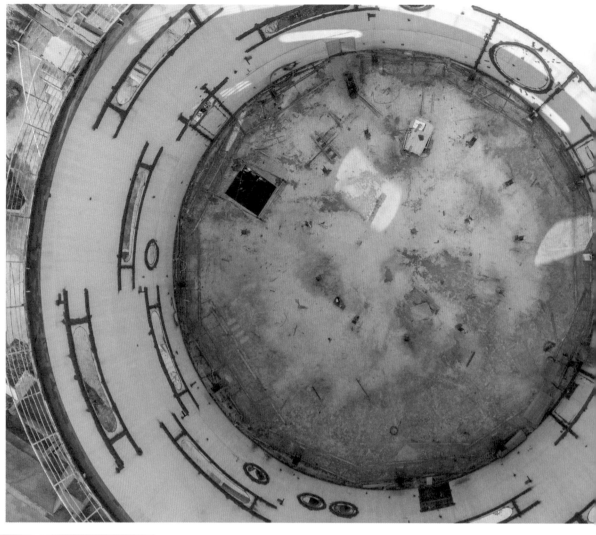

Cuts on the thick plates of steel (right); the new structure added in the tank (below); the gap between the Super-Surface and the tank (opposite).

Despite the museum's relaxed and easy-going atmosphere, the project presented a number of physical and logistical challenges.

For instance, not only is the architectural structure and circular shape of the tanks unusual, but the architects had to maintain the structural integrity of the old oil tanks while connecting them to the new underground spaces. As Li Hu explains:

> Although they were originally made of thick plates of steel, and are very strong structures, the structural engineers decided that no new configuration was to be supported by the tanks as a precautionary measure, since they were not able to model and simulate the load-bearing capacities of the old tanks precisely.

This meant that new additions, including the Super-Surface, could only lightly 'touch' the tanks without adding any load. "We had to convert a space that was not originally built for people into one suitable for ongoing human use," Li Hu says, "and to decide how to carry out the construction given all of these constraints."

The architects also had to negotiate the boundary of the site, with an adjacent heliport to the north, and strict structural requirements imposed by a cross-river vehicular tunnel, which passes diagonally beneath. Since the tunnel authorities would not permit any change in the weight of the deep soil layer above and around the tunnel, this meant that the new construction could not encroach on the area of protection designated for the tunnel.

Thus, the architects found themselves negotiating with a multitude of government authorities, from the tunnel, aviation, and port officials to the parking department.

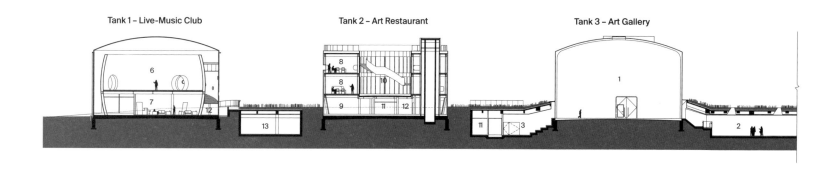

Tank 1 – Live-Music Club   Tank 2 – Art Restaurant   Tank 3 – Art Gallery

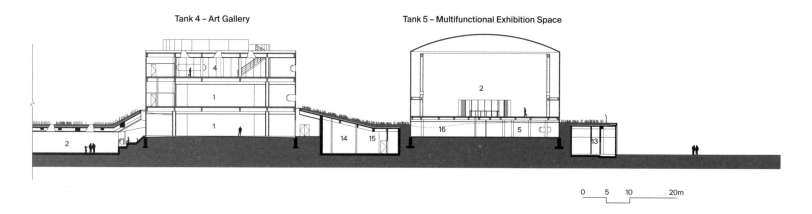

Tank 4 – Art Gallery   Tank 5 – Multifunctional Exhibition Space

0   5   10   20m

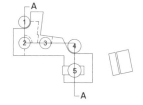

Overall Section A

1   Art gallery
2   Multifunctional space
3   Café
4   Office
5   Open office
6   Live music club
7   Bar
8   Restaurant
9   Kitchen
10 Atrium
11 Restroom
12 Facilities room
13 Service
14 Security services
15 Locker room
16 HVAC

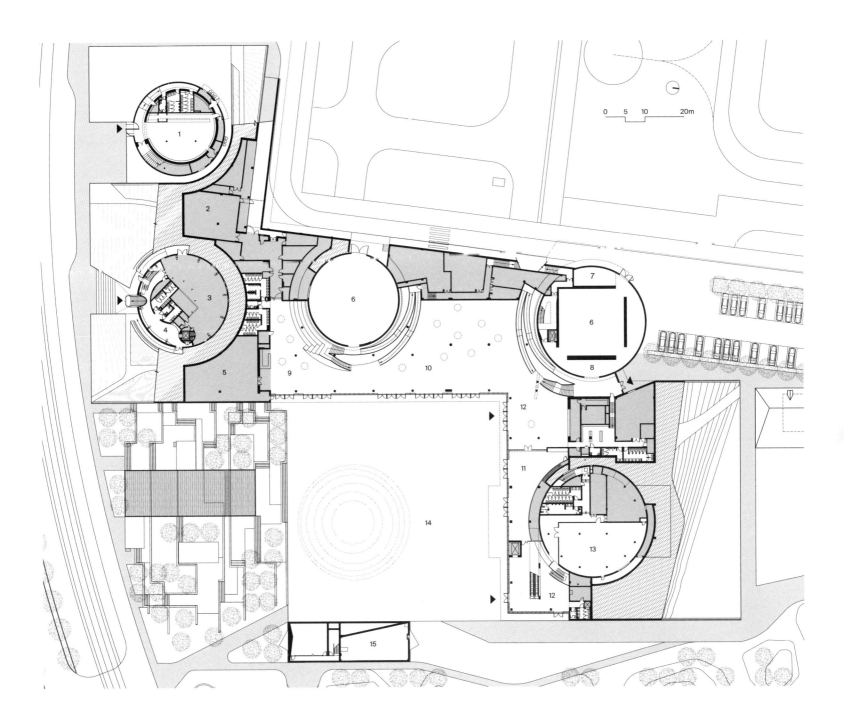

Ground-floor Plan

1 Bar
2 Art storage
3 Kitchen
4 Lobby
5 Lecture hall
6 Art gallery
7 Preparation
8 Foyer
9 Café
10 Multifunctional space
11 Museum shop
12 Lobby
13 Open-plan office/art studio
14 Urban plaza
15 Service

From the beginning of the project, the programme was open-ended, and the design brief revised many times in order to determine the most pertinent, sustainable, and viable use for the site. The original brief was to convert the tanks into theatres, as part of a centre for the performing arts, but, after a year, that idea was abandoned when a large site nearby was designated for development as a theatre.

A sketch by Li Hu demonstrating the revised design brief (below); sketches by Li Hu (opposite).

"Tank Shanghai is representative of the fluid situation we work in, in China. We seldom receive a very clear brief, and the planned use often changes. It can all be indefinite," says Li Hu.

For most of the design process, the architects did not know who would be operating the site, so functional flexibility was central to their planning.

Then, in March 2016, the developer started collaborating with Mr Qiao, one of the first modern contemporary collectors in China, whose collection of over 500 pieces includes work by Sterling Ruby, Martin Creed, Olafur Eliasson, and Zeng Fanzhi.

"Things keep changing—that is the reality we work with in a fast-developing country," says Wenjing. "But, luckily, when Qiao came on board, the planning we had already done gave him sufficient flexibility and variety, and he made no big changes other than to delay building the design shop."

"The objective has to be stable and focused, but how we achieve it can be very fluid, like a liquid before it gels," Wenjing explains.

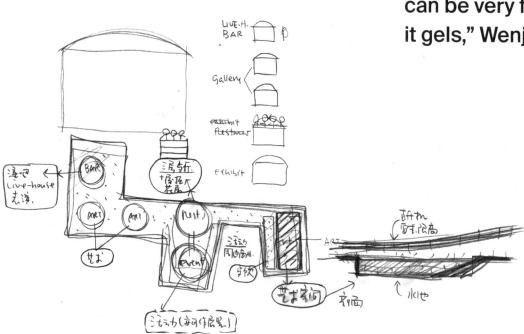

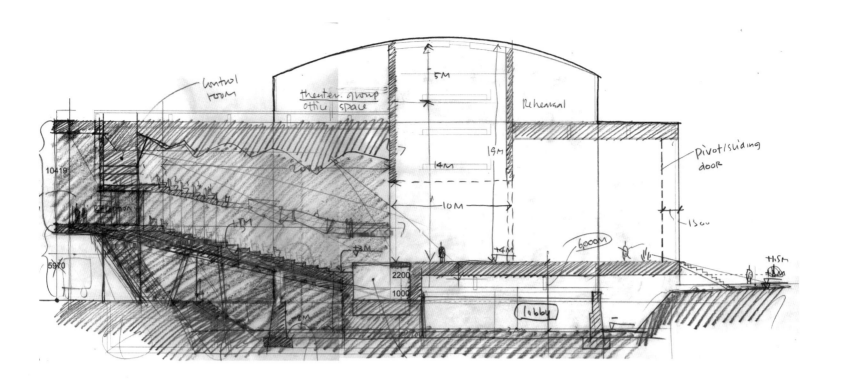

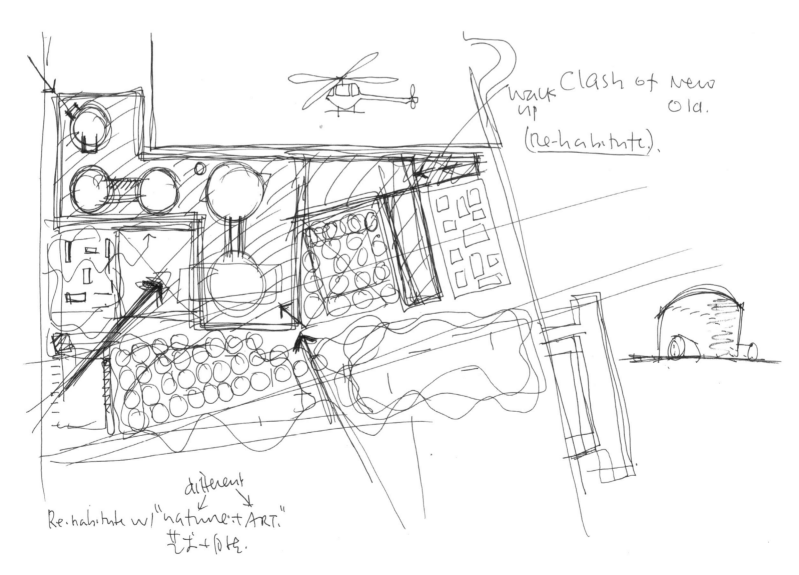

"We were motivated by the idea of shaping a new type of art institution that is as open, generous, and accessible as a modern park; where art and culture encourage people to relax and enjoy the outdoors."

The architects especially admire institutions such as the Louisiana Museum in Denmark, where the understated modernist building complex, designed by Danish architects Jørgen Bo and Vilhelm Wohlert in the 1950s, fits naturally into the terrain, as well as great urban parks such as New York City's Central Park.

"It provides a sanctuary for people and nature, and, at the same time, it is a social equaliser that attracts and generously accommodates all walks of life," they say. An unconventional art institution that is simultaneously an art centre and a public park, instead of a museum in a park, is, therefore, central to the concept. The architects wanted visitors to be attracted first by an open and inviting landscape of tall grasses, trees, water features, and birdlife, and then, almost incidentally, to discover the exhibition and event spaces either underneath or integrated with nature.

Keen to avoid any impression of a bordered site, Li Hu and Wenjing formulated the design concept around long, sloping landscaped meadows that lead down to and around each tank gallery, offering open access to the street and riverside, so that visitors can move freely between the city, nature, and art.

The result is the subtle merging of architecture and landscape throughout the Z-shaped Super-Surface—a five-hectare landscaped park on a concrete roof that connects three of the five tanks combining the site's disparate elements. Visitors arriving from the street walk down a pebble path through a terraced waterscape towards a central plaza and the main entrance, which is tucked into the slope so naturally that they may hardly notice they are below ground.

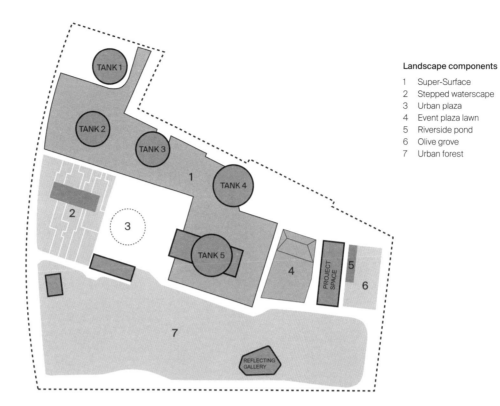

Landscape components

1 Super-Surface
2 Stepped waterscape
3 Urban plaza
4 Event plaza lawn
5 Riverside pond
6 Olive grove
7 Urban forest

The long, sloping landscape that leads down to and around the tanks (opposite); a diagram of the landscape elements (right); an aerial view of the park (below).

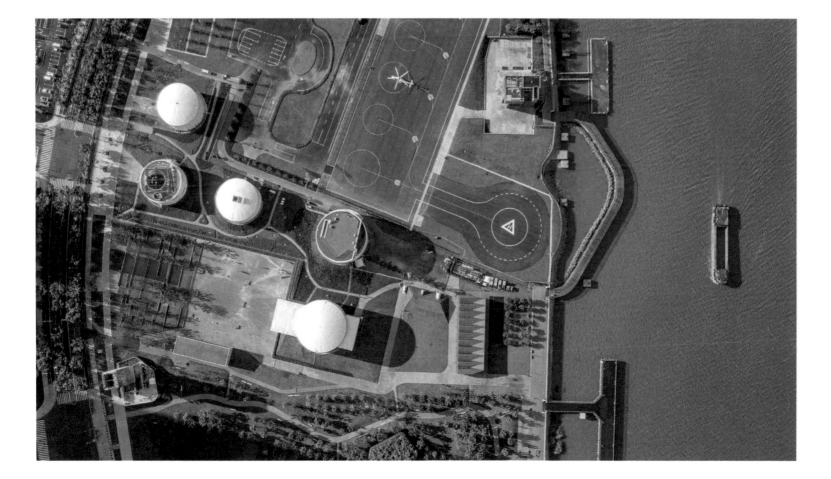

"We see the project as building an ecosystem, and the site as an urban park to be experienced as a place rather than architecture," Li Hu clarifies.

The 'urban forest' flanks the southern side of the plaza, providing greenery and shade for residents. The eastern part of the site has a second grassy plaza for outdoor events and leisure, and for standing room at music festivals.

The Super-Surface is dotted with a collection of art installations and, underground, a newly constructed, open-plan level connects three of the tank galleries. There are event venues, a restaurant and café, a live music club, museum offices, and art storage.

The design is taken from traditional Chinese landscape paintings, where man-made structures disappear into the landscape. "The architecture we create doesn't have to be the assertive object in the project. We give priority to nature and the tanks— the industrial past and the memories. Our real creation is hidden," Li Hu and Wenjing explain.

The urban forest (left and opposite).

The original industrial aesthetic of the tanks has been carefully preserved, and the architectural interventions limited to the occasional capsule-shaped opening and porthole needed to light the interior.

The museum is a brand-new institution, and its long-term plan is to show both Chinese and international contemporary works. Li Hu and Wenjing approached the interior design of each of the five tanks differently, allowing for a diversity of art and art forms.

"How you encounter art can be quite different at Tank Shanghai. You may spot a round skylight in the tall grasses, through which you have a glimpse of the exhibition below. Or you may walk right up to the windows to look inside the main hall. Art surprises and welcomes you here," Wenjing explains.

The opening towards the Huangpu River (top left); a skylight (left); steps integrated with seating (opposite); the partial view of the tanks (overleaf).

Tank 1 and Tank 2 provide supporting functions that generate revenue, and can be used for promotional events: Tank 1 is a two-storey bar with space for live music performances, and an added inner drum-shaped volume for acoustics; Tank 2 is a restaurant in a round central courtyard with a roofdeck for alfresco dining, reached by a circular staircase.

Tank 3 is deliberately kept empty to preserve the raw power that the two architects felt from the space during their initial visits. It is almost unchanged, except for the addition of a large central oculus, fireproofing, and acoustic materials that meet safety and technical requirements, and will display large artworks and installations. A retractable skylight above the oculus allows wind and rain into the gallery if desired, as was the case for the opening exhibition and solo show by Argentinian artist Adrián Villar Rojas.

"The sound is amazing. It does not die away quickly—it goes around and around," says Li Hu.

Tank 2 (top); Tank 3 (above); Tank 1 (right); axonometric drawings of Tank 1, Tank 2, and Tank 3 (opposite).

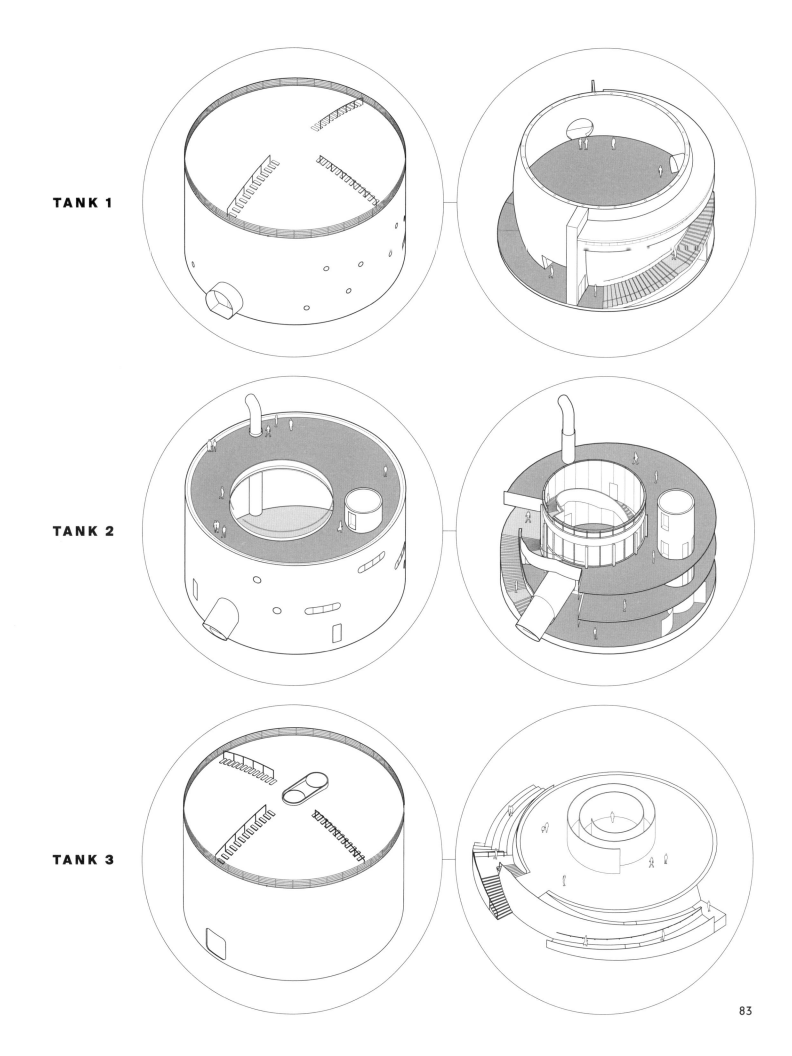

TANK 1

TANK 2

TANK 3

83

The gallery in Tank 4 (above);
axonometric drawings of Tank 4
and Tank 5 (opposite);
the Tank 5 stage, which faces the
event-plaza lawn (overleaf).

In Tank 4, the architects inserted a three-level white box that offers a more conventional space to display paintings. Finally, Tank 5 has a rectangle piercing the body of the original structure, emerging on either side to form stages for outdoor events without disturbing the buildings' aesthetic integrity.

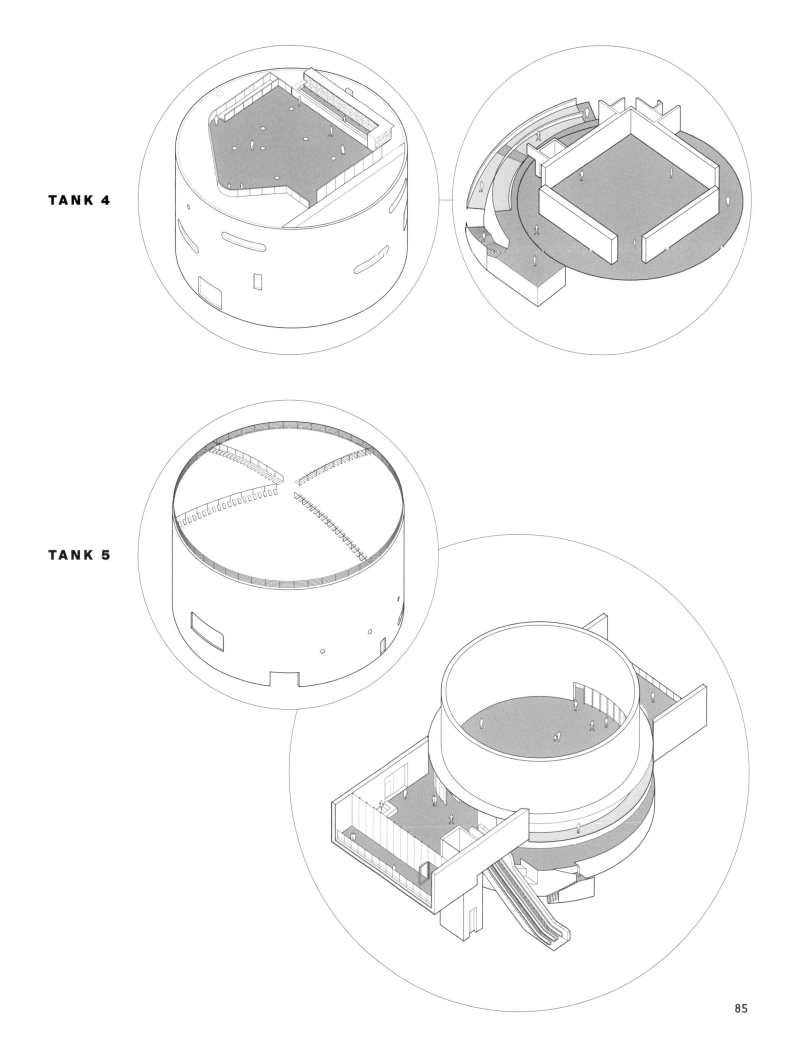

TANK 4

TANK 5

Li Hu and Wenjing's Super-Surface, which connects four of the tanks, has a landscaped concrete roof with sculpture and flower gardens above a continuous open floor.

Visitors enter the art museum through a public plaza, where hidden misting devices create a cooling, foggy microclimate in summer. They are planted in a large circle, which brings to mind a sixth tank, demolished when the neighbouring heliport was built.

Inside, the walls of the open-plan floor are clad in simple white concrete with slender columns that allow for fluid, natural circulation of people around the space. Each tank has a concrete and thick steel-plate ramp whose complex tapered form follows the geometry of the tank's foundation, which had to remain intact. A slim skylight strip between the tank and the new concrete roof lets in the daylight while maintaining the independence of both the new and old structures, ensuring that they do not actually touch each other.

"Bringing the existing and new elements together, with the potential to transform ways of seeing and knowing, was a joy to us," says Wenjing.

On the Super-Surface (above left);
the ramp to Tank 3 (above);
the mist feature in the urban plaza
(far left); the open space under
the Super-Surface (left).

Creating a public park that covers most of the Tank site suggests a new way of experiencing art, one that allows people to move freely between nature and art. The integrated whole is socially inclusive in that the entire complex welcomes a family picnic as warmly as a fashion show, a festival, or an exhibition—or all of these things at once.

"A museum is designed to bring art to people, and the park gathers people together too, so there is a symbiotic connection where art becomes the context of the park," Li Hu explains.

Restoring the riverfront ecology is central to the project. People, vegetation, birds, and insects have all returned to what was once a derelict post-industrial site, and the lush, thickly planted, undulating landscape provides much-needed parkland in a city where less than twenty percent of the surface area is green space.

A bird's-eye view of Tank Shanghai (right).

In the surrounding landscape are two separate, smaller galleries designed late in the project: Project Space, in the footprint of a demolished pump room, and the Reflecting Gallery, which contains municipal community service functions.

Project Space provides shelter for visitors (above); Project Space (right).

The Reflecting Gallery (far left); misting devices in the urban plaza (left).

Wrapped in polished stainless-steel sheets, the Reflecting Gallery reflects the greenery around it, and dissolves almost entirely into the surrounding urban forest. The multipurpose Project Space overlooks the river and a pool that remains from the old airport. Its water would have been used by firefighters then, but now it is a rectangular reflecting pond surrounded by olive trees. Project Space's roofline is saw-toothed, and intentionally contrasts with the curvilinearity of the tanks.

"People come here for the park, and are happily surprised by the art and architecture," says Wenjing. "They don't see architecture at first: instead there is the unexpected magic of the tanks, trees, and grass. Art is in the wonder of discovery, as it should be in life."

Since opening in March 2019, Tank Shanghai has already attracted nearly a million visitors, and introduced new audiences to traditionally closed-off arts centres.

The architects' sensitive approach to a coherent, open museum, where visitors stroll through a park, has already attracted high-profile exhibitions, book fairs, and AI conferences.

Thus, Tank Shanghai represents a model for the future, and a new type of urban art institution that stands in powerful contrast to exclusive cultural projects. It links past and future, fusing art with nature, and, even more importantly, establishes meaningful connections between people and collective, inclusive cultural spaces.

The architects are particularly pleased with the organic feel of Tank Shanghai:

It was such a complex project, and there were so many challenges from all fronts, but the outcome looks natural, and its relaxed feel appeals to the public, as if it had always been there. It is very important to us to make something complicated look simple.

"We greatly appreciate the ancient Chinese scholar Laozi's description of the virtue of water, which benefits everything but competes with nothing," Wenjing says. "Here, architecture is the facilitator, synthesising everything else into a coherent and seemingly effortless whole."

"This project changed our perception of when a building is 'finished.' Two years into the operation, and Tank Shanghai is still not finished," Wenjing continues, "at least not according to our design drawings." Two of the tank interiors remain in a raw, unfinished state due to funding constraints, yet amazingly successful fashion shows and digital art exhibitions have been held here. Established cultural and architectural traditions are being revised almost everywhere, and OPEN are optimistic that the trinity of architecture, nature, and art will continue to evolve.

"We may come back in five years and find it looking very different. Art has this amazing transformative power," they say.

Events and activities held at Tank Shanghai since its opening (opposite); Tank Shanghai in the dusk (overleaf).

Shenzhen, China

PINGSHAN PERFORMING ARTS CENTRE

In a new urban district in northeast Shenzhen, culture and community share centre stage at the Pingshan Performing Arts Centre, where they challenge architectural conventions in a deceptively simple building.

Due to the relative freedom of China's fast-developing urban landscape, and with the opportunity to maximise and engage in the creative power of civic architecture, Li Hu and Wenjing suggested reinventing their client's initial brief and were able to propose innovative designs. The architects gave the project a nickname that has stuck, and is even used by the operator in their official publications: the Drama Box.

So, instead of the single, massive grand theatre that was originally planned, the architects designed a new, dynamic civic centre that would act as a cultural hybrid, incorporating multiple uses and activities, with functional spaces for rehearsals and performances alongside educational and social programmes. The architectural strategy included a restaurant, a café, and a bar, as well as a public promenade and lush, landscaped public gardens that would be integrated within the building—all of which would encourage locals to use the centre regularly.

Because the architects believe it is important to not be unnecessarily extravagant when it comes to design, particularly when spending public money on cultural buildings, they took a critical look at the recent proliferation of contemporary theatres across China, examining about thirty in detail.

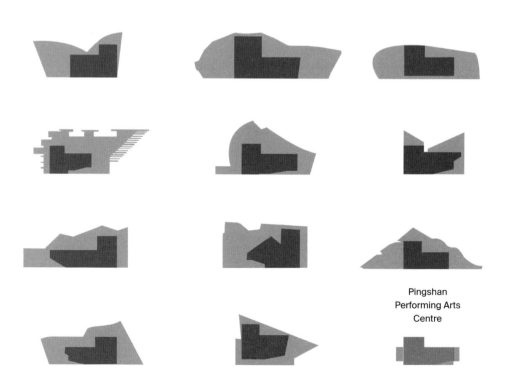

Pingshan
Performing Arts
Centre

The northeast corner of the building (opening page); a study of existing grand-theatre typologies (right).

This proved illuminating, as Wenjing points out:

> Most theatres built in the last few years in China have lavish, monumental exteriors, but inside they are often spatially monotonous and detached from the community and everyday urban life. That they underutilise the tremendous public resources invested in them is an understatement for many of these theatres.

They were also struck by how the core theatre component often remains the same simple form, irrespective of the flamboyance of the external shell:

"A lot of theatre buildings may appear visually exciting from the outside, but inside the main element—the theatre—often stays remarkably similar, as does the experience of the actors and audience."

Realising this, Li Hu and Wenjing wanted to design a simple, welcoming, flexible structure with no outward iconography, and to redirect the sophistication into the interior, which people truly inhabit.

> A cultural building like the Pingshan Performing Arts Centre requires a relatively large investment, and we wanted to maximise its 'effectiveness' as a public place. Most of the theatres we have looked at in China function purely as theatres and they are empty when there is no programme, which is, essentially, most of the time, as there are a number of theatres popping up in China and, currently, there are not always enough performances to fill them. We wanted to avoid this, especially since the centre is in a relatively recently developed district and needs to attract a new, local audience.

THE DESIGN CONCEPT

The Drama Box is a 23,500-square-metre project. At the heart of the building is the 1,200-seat Grand Theatre, enclosed in dark reddish, engineered wood panels. Next to the Grand Theatre is a smaller 150-seat 'Black Box' theatre. Elsewhere, intricately wrapped around the Grand Theatre like pieces of a puzzle, practice rooms, dance rooms, educational spaces, and services occupy the five floors of the building, along with informal spaces for the public, such as viewing balconies, an outdoor theatre, a café, and a restaurant with a bar and lounge. There is parking in the basement.

"What we mean when we say Drama Box is in reference to Chinese treasure boxes that, when closed, appear simple and unassuming, yet when they are opened reveal a sophisticated interior, storing rare treasures. We felt that this different interpretation of sophistication encapsulates what we wanted to achieve on an architectural scale," Li Hu explains.

A diagram of the Drama Box (below).

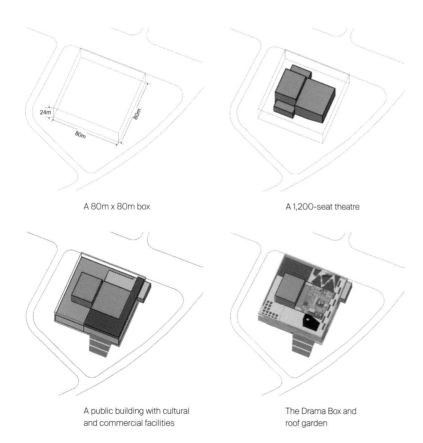

A 80m x 80m box

A 1,200-seat theatre

A public building with cultural and commercial facilities

The Drama Box and roof garden

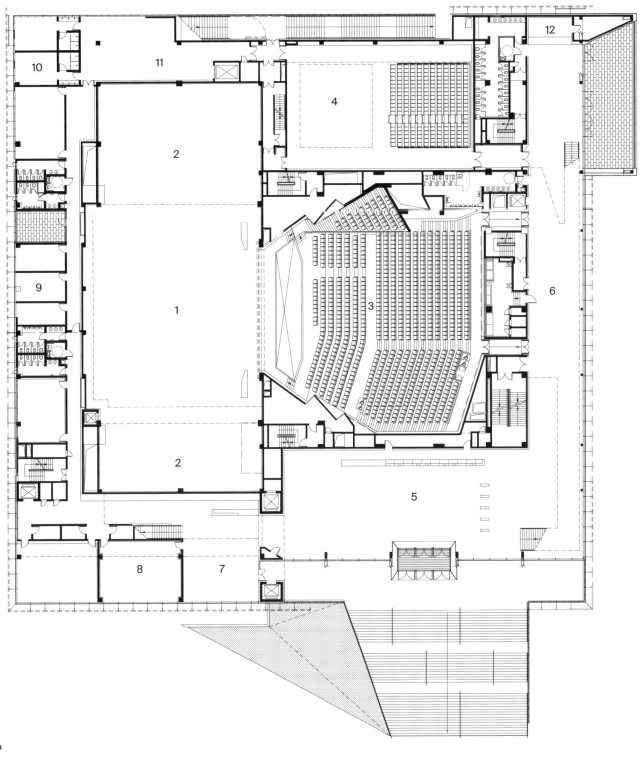

Lobby-level Plan

1 Stage
2 Stage wing
3 Auditorium
4 Black Box theatre
5 Lobby of Pingshan Performing Arts Centre
6 Lounge
7 Lobby of Experience Centre
8 Dance Studio
9 Office
10 Dressing room
11 Service space
12 Bar

0   5   10   20m

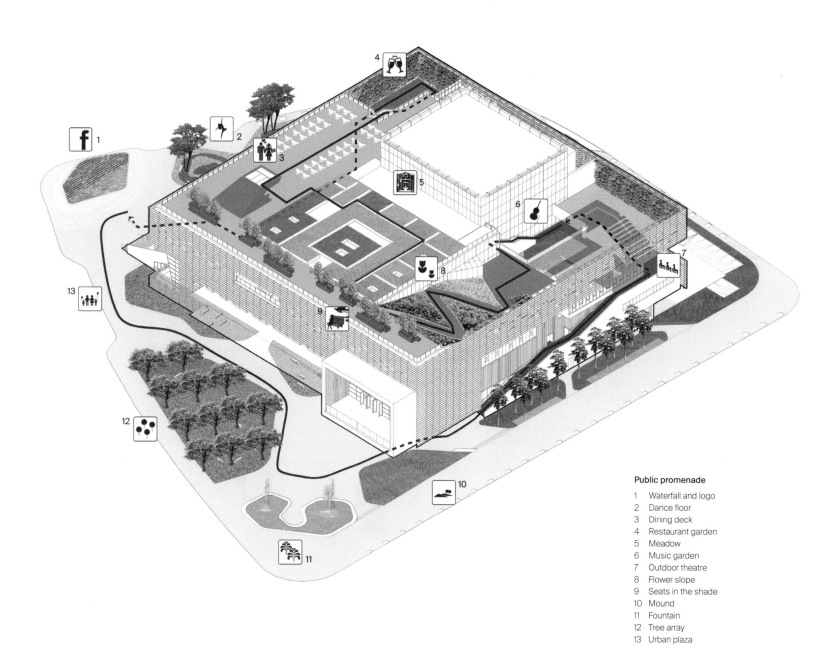

Public promenade

1   Waterfall and logo
2   Dance floor
3   Dining deck
4   Restaurant garden
5   Meadow
6   Music garden
7   Outdoor theatre
8   Flower slope
9   Seats in the shade
10 Mound
11 Fountain
12 Tree array
13 Urban plaza

A diagram of the public promenade
(above); activities taking place on the
urban plaza (opposite).

A stepped approach from the southern outdoor plaza leads visitors to the main entrance and an airy, double-height lobby. A warm palette of materials and abundant natural light combine to create a relaxed and welcoming ambience. The wood panels contrast with the light-toned floor and ceiling leading up to the Grand Theatre.

"Our main goal was a cultural hub and a building that connects people as a community, rather than a superficially dramatic, standalone architectural object," says Wenjing.

The volume of the Grand Theatre, wrapped in dark, red-toned wood panels (opposite); the main lobby (below).

The urban plaza (above); the outdoor theatre (top right).

Li Hu recalls visiting Pingshan a decade ago, when it was still semi-rural. Formerly a group of fishing villages north of Hong Kong, in 1980, Shenzhen was named China's first Special Economic Zone, and has since grown rapidly into a manufacturing megalopolis—a modern hub for tech and electronics companies, and an area that is fast developing a considerable reputation as a design powerhouse.

As it attracts a younger, more educated workforce, Shenzhen's urban footprint is expanding to outskirts like Pingshan, where factories that develop advanced lithium batteries and electric cars are based. As the area becomes more established, the local government responsible for its future is actively encouraging a strong cultural core of libraries, museums, and theatres.

Breaking away from the single-function, cultural-landmark typology to supply the non-theatre-going public with a new cultural hub sets an example of social inclusivity for civic buildings. It also makes the centre more sustainable, functional, and effective.

We do not believe a theatre necessarily requires a dramatic structure, but it should be relevant, and it is only common sense that rich and exciting experiences—both spatial and functional—will help a public building to engage with the larger community.

Fortunately, their client, the municipal government, understood what they wanted to achieve. Li Hu explains:

We were lucky because they understood how important culture is to the community, and they listened to and supported our proposals, including adding a café and a restaurant to make operating the building commercially viable. They even adjusted the urban zoning for this particular site to permit some commercial spaces so that the revenue-generating facilities we proposed could be achieved.

A cantilever creates shade for the urban plaza (far left); the misting forest (left).

As a result, the new centre brings together contradictory elements: the formal, elite world of traditional theatre and the more relaxed, experimental avant-garde that serves a wider audience.

For instance, the architects made the rehearsal room from the original brief into the smaller, more flexible Black Box, which, due to its versatility and size, is used much more often than the Grand Theatre. And there are plenty of multiple-use workrooms for music and dance lessons, and practising. These rooms are accessible both by corridors inside the building and through a winding outdoor promenade, which is open to the public even when the Grand Theatre is closed.

The Black Box theatre (opposite);
the dance studio (below).

The architects explain: Theatre is a
very sophisticated building typology,
and we must respect the way the building
functions, from ticketing to back-of-house
and rehearsals. Yet, at the same time, we
want to provide access so that the public
gets to enjoy the facilities and outdoor
spaces freely, including wandering up to
the roof gardens. The need to offer free
access and a controlled entrance to the
space can, at times, exert contradictory
and opposing forces. However, through
design, we carefully resolved this added
complexity in the placement of the public
routes and access points, and we were able
to both achieve openness to the public
and maintain restricted areas for ticket
holders and back-of-house functions so
that, in the end, they actually complement
instead of contradict each other.

At the time the architects began designing the centre, no operator had been appointed. Luckily, OPEN was able to assemble a group of expert theatre consultants, each with special technical expertise and years of experience. Practical advice from Mr Tan Siying, a retired director of the local Shenzhen Grand Theatre and an advisor to the government, proved invaluable in the early days. He was also the one who immediately embraced the architects' idea to include a café and restaurant to make the centre more sustainable from the operational perspective. Huang Zhanchun, the acoustic and theatre consultant, and Huang Zhigao, an experienced stage director, helped to make sure the theatre met state-of-the-art performance requirements. When the operator finally came on board, not long before the building was completed, they found the building so functionally sound that almost no alterations were needed.

In a major departure from classic theatre design, Li Hu and Wenjing made the Grand Theatre's seating asymmetrical, with two interconnected tiers so actors are able to move from the mezzanine to the orchestra level and onto the stage, allowing new forms of performance as well as immersive and interactive audience participation:

"It was tricky because, while we wanted to explore a different seating arrangement to suit a wider variety of performances, actors need a clear sense of the central line in the theatre. We had to maintain this critical visual balance with our asymmetrical design."

Grand Theatre (left).

Li Hu and Wenjing believe in design that blurs boundaries between the interior of a building and the outside. The centre's cantilevers make the structure appear to float above the ground, and the face is 'punched open' to reveal the view. A large, ten-metre-deep cantilever over the eastern side of the plaza affords comfortable cover from the heat and rain.

The envelope around the main building is a glass curtain wall with perforated aluminium shading devices that balance transparency and views with additional opportunities to shelter from the heat. These precision-engineered, V-shaped panels are a direct response to the local climate: they protect the building from exposure to the sun, and improve natural ventilation. The upper part of the panels has fewer perforations, and largely blocks out the unwanted direct sunlight, while the lower part is more open, encouraging visitors to enjoy the view.

The perforated aluminum V sections (below); the public promenade on the north side of the building (right).

Internally, the use of natural wood and bamboo engages with the landscape and the kinds of plants that grew on that site at one time, making the performance spaces more connected with their context. These materials are juxtaposed with blue corrugated-metal panels in a combination that also reflects the character of Pingshan District's industries. The deep blue of the textured interior walls of the Grand Theatre contrasts with the warm yellow bamboo panels that are used on the ceiling, and on the backs of seats.

"Blue is our way of paying tribute to Shenzhen as a subtropical metropolis on the sea, and blue is also the main colour in a traditional, local Hakka fabric," Wenjing explains:

To keep this blue for the theatre interior was actually one of the many things that we had to fight hard for all the way, and well into the construction phase. Initially, our client asked for a traditional, red-toned interior, but, for this site and its context, we liked this distinctive blue when set against the warm bamboo panels.

The brighter, more vibrant blue on the corrugated metal-clad walls and ceiling of the Black Box theatre lobby, and on the outside by the promenade, distinguishes between and complements the otherwise muted colours used in the rest of the building.

The side balcony in the grand theatre (opposite); the lounge outside the Black Box theatre (left).

The music patio (right); the outdoor theatre at the northwest corner of the building (opposite).

To inject a sense of energy and purpose, the projecting level above the plaza and the small outdoor theatre have vibrant red soffits, and the outdoor plaza doubles as an informal theatre. There are landscaped gardens throughout the building and on the roof. The public promenade that links the gardens takes different ascending forms: sometimes it is as narrow as a staircase, in other places it is wider and serves as an impromptu outdoor theatre; elsewhere it zigzags to mitigate the vertical hike to otherwise hard-to-reach areas of the building. In the public plaza, granite benches, fountains, and the misting system encourage people of all ages to stop and sit, or play. This is a key part of the overall design, which is further complemented by the welcoming shady area that is cast by the large cantilever on the east elevation. From past experience, the architects understand perfectly how to use shade and ventilation to temper Shenzhen's hot, humid summers.

"The outdoor space is used for everything from dancing and exercises to kung fu in the plaza," Li Hu says. "People even lie down on the benches to take a nap in the shade on hot summer days."

The urban plaza (opposite left, far left, left); the roof garden (above left, above).

The rooftop garden (right); an aerial view of the roof garden (opposite).

Throughout the building, the interweaving and vegetation slowly reveal themselves, giving visitors a constantly changing prospect as they walk along the promenade from the ground-floor plaza to the landscaped roof garden. With a limited budget, and an affinity for all things natural, the architects worked with the landscape designer to choose wild-looking vegetation that requires little maintenance. At first sight, the field of tall grass on the rooftop seems to be a prairie, in dramatic variance to the encircling modern housing towers. Planters on the roof terrace also double as seating, so people can sit there and unwind. The architects chose red frangipani (*Plumeria rubra*) for shade as it is resilient enough to survive the frequent typhoons.

The roof garden reduces the heat in the building and provides panoramic views of the city below, a world away from the theatre.

The road curving around the building defines the interface of the site from the surrounding urban area, and has allowed OPEN to focus on building connections to the park on the east side and the residential communities to the south and west.

"We feel very strongly that nature should not be treated as an accessory. We like integrated open spaces that people can inhabit and be part of, where they feel comfortable being themselves."

"In China, we tend to have to deal with a lot more challenges, because the context of building here can be fluid," Li Hu explains:

> Sometimes a contractor makes a mistake and, because of the schedule, there is no time to tear down and rebuild. Sometimes the client may change their mind. Or, in the case of Pingshan, the curtain-wall building code was suddenly changed in the middle of the design process. You have to remain cautiously flexible and be quick to come up with solutions to work around unexpected problems.

> It is hard for outsiders to imagine, but, basically, this means that your work is never finished, even after completing all the design drawings. You may begin with one thing and end up with something a little different, but we have learned to deal with the problems— and sometimes you end up with something even better.

Li Hu says that, at a conceptual and detailed level, their designs are often a reaction to what is happening around them and, instinctively, they question whether an architectural typology that works in the West would be appropriate in China:

> The country is in an ideal position to innovate. We feel strongly that many established and taken-for-granted architectural typologies— most of which have been established by Europeans—need to be re-examined to allow for the complexity of urban and cultural life nowadays.

The east side view at night (right); the Grand Theatre auditorium (overleaf).

The architects do not claim to have a definitive answer, but they believe it is time to critically rethink what is appropriate for China; to be mindful of its cultural heritage, but not be shackled by it, and to build with compassion and vision for the future. Essentially, the theatre should relate to everyone, even people who are not traditional theatre-goers, or those who simply cannot afford to go.

"The centre is the antithesis of most of China's huge, expensive theatres. It is not a grand empty shell, but it is a humble part of everyday urban life," says Li Hu. "This is our counterstatement: here, everyone can experience and explore drama inside the box."

SHANGHAI QINGPU PINGHE INTERNATIONAL SCHOOL

BIBLIO-THEATRE

'Bibliotheatre' is the name Li Hu and Wenjing have devised to describe their intricate Chinese-puzzle-like combination of library, theatre, and 'black box' (an indoor performance space with plain black walls and a level floor) in a single building. It stands on the most visible corner of the site of the Shanghai Qingpu Pinghe International School, where the architects have created an inviting campus for 2,000 students. The commanding position it takes presents OPEN's vision of a school with culture at the heart of the curriculum.

Students affectionately refer to the vivid blue building as 'the blue whale,' and its friendly, zoomorphic appearance presents a novel blend of form, materiality, and culture, suggesting a new, multi-layered architectural framework for education—a world away from the megastructure typology that usually dominates China's learning landscape.

The entrance to the theatre (opening page); the south side of the Bibliotheatre (right).

THE SITE

According to Li Hu, although the original commission to design a school complete with all supporting facilities for students aged from three to fifteen was relatively straightforward, at first they thought the project would be almost impossible to achieve within the tight timeframe. The local government, which had released the land for educational use, had given the developer, OPEN's client Mr Li Shifeng, just two years to design, build, and open the school. Even with China's famed fast pace of construction, a campus of this scale would normally take about four years from design to completion.

In recent years, demand in China for private school education that offers an international curriculum has grown at an exponential rate. Qingpu, a new district of metropolitan Shanghai, is an excellent example of how an agricultural district has been rapidly urbanised, with communities in new, high-rise, mixed-use districts in need of educational facilities.

Their client, Mr Li, who had studied in the United States and has a passion for education, had seen OPEN's widely publicised Garden School in Beijing, which opened in 2014, where Li Hu and Wenjing had designed a natural, open-air setting for students in order to maximise contact with nature in the dense urban location. They did this by submerging some of the school's larger communal facilities, such as the canteen, auditorium, gymnasium, and swimming pool, half below ground, which allowed for gardens to be planted on their rooftops.

The Garden School in Beijing (right); a bird's-eye view of the school as a village (opposite).

Mr Li hoped that a simpler, pared-down version could be constructed on the Shanghai site in time. However, Li Hu and Wenjing did not want to simply replicate something that they had designed in a completely different context, especially since the age range at this new school is much greater than the Beijing one and, therefore, the needs of the students are more complex. They also wanted to break away from their Garden School megastructure approach, which has been widely, often mindlessly, adopted by other new schools that have popped up all over the country.

Li Hu and Wenjing decided that the only practical solution was to deconstruct the traditional school programme by grouping it into smaller, separate buildings, and forming a village-like campus. In addition, to further plan and compress the erection process, multiple contractors were allowed to work on site at the same time.

"Even though our client was expecting a simple plan, and we were suggesting something more elaborate, he understood what design would add to the learning environment, and he was completely supportive of the new proposal," Li Hu says.

The architects' thoughtful, holistic approach to learning has worked equally well for the wider campus. Li Hu and Wenjing have school-age children of their own, and so they know that reading, art, and sports are not often prioritised in the learning system. They explain:

These subjects don't usually contribute to student scores, but we believe they are an essential foundation for a well-rounded person and their well-being in the future. So, even at the earliest design stage, we thought about how to increase the presence of these subjects, and this is when we started to develop the idea of integrating such cultural functions within a 'bibliotheatre.'

For the master plan of the 50,350-square-metre school site, Li Hu and Wenjing understood their challenge was to produce a village settlement-like campus on an urban plot with limited land. They began by considering different ways of defining and arranging the classrooms, dormitories, and administrative offices, as well as the art, culture, and sports facilities, while also exploring how a normally concentrated area for sports could be broken down into several sports fields, gardens, and running trails across the site.

A bird's-eye view of the campus (above left); the running trail between the sports centre and the art building (left); a running trail between classroom Learning Cubes (opposite).

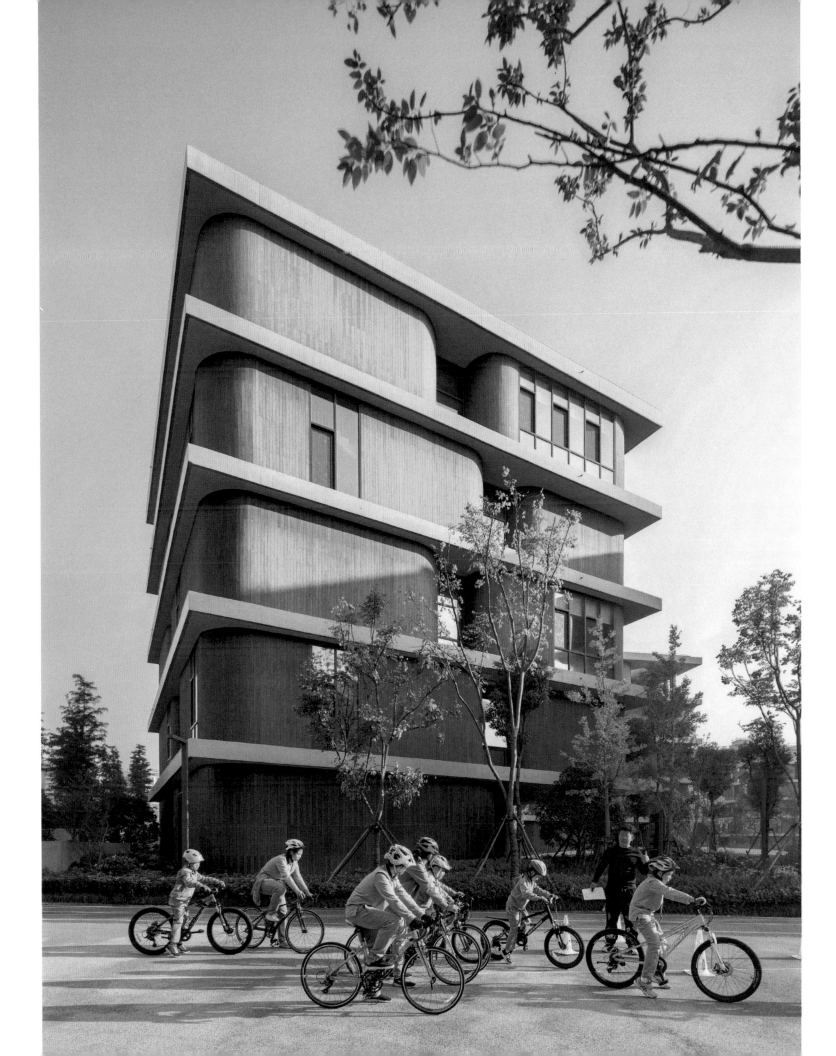

"After looking at more than thirty plans for how the site could work, I realised that if we did not discard concepts of educational architecture from the past, we would never be able to move beyond them or to think innovatively about the experience of a campus," Li Hu explains. "A school's open spaces are as important as the buildings, if not more so. Kids need trees, grass, insects, and to be able to run around and expend their energy in a stimulating environment."

The outdoor spaces and landscape elements among the buildings.

The sports centre (right);
the kindergarten building (below);
the art building (far right).

Wenjing recalls how they thought very carefully about the ways in which the different classes would use the school. "We wanted to assess how they move about the campus, and how views and linkages could help with this," she says. Both architects believe that it is important for buildings to have a distinctive character. The result here is a mix of different forms, styles, colours, and heights, offering a compressed yet rich context that makes it easy for students to identify each building.

"I see it as a combination of fairy tales and rationality," Li Hu explains:

It's a fairy tale in that each building has a hidden analogy. For instance, the classroom 'Learning Cubes' are like houses, and we wanted the largest cube, for the gym, swimming pool, and canteen, to feel light, and so that building looks like bubbles. The art building resembles a strange crystal, while the friendly, welcoming blue form of the Bibliotheatre stands out.

The basketball courts (below); a lawn between Learning Cubes (right); the sports field (far right); the pond (bottom).

The buildings are woven together by the outdoor spaces: sports grounds and playgrounds, gardens, lawns, a forest, ponds, and a plaza. "This is a city school, but the grounds have something reminiscent of traditional Chinese scholars' gardens. We were inspired by small parcels of land that hint at a larger prospect within a condensed terrain—setting up layers of a landscape in a limited space," Wenjing says.

Breaking down the scale of the sports and park areas proved a practical, functional solution to Shanghai's hot and humid climate, by creating shady spots between buildings.

"The landscape and the distance between buildings shape a subtle magnetic field of attractions, like people in a room talking to each other in a relaxed ambience," Li Hu adds.

Li Hu and Wenjing are guided by nature, and their initial inspiration for the Bibliotheatre, with its many spiky skylights, was a sea cucumber. The unusual colour comes from fond memories of blue sea stars that they saw on the ocean floor while on holiday in Guam. "That particular, deep blue is ingrained in my mind. It is a bold colour that changes with the weather, and in sunlight it produces a powerful emotion. It also contrasts nicely with the warm bamboo-clad Learning Cubes and with the white bubble form of the nearby sports centre," Li Hu explains.

Both Li Hu and Wenjing are happy that their original intention has evolved into a friendly-looking animal in the students' eyes. "The blue whale is a nice analogy," Li Hu observes. "The cantilevered entrance looks like a whale's open mouth. I like how it has an interesting appearance."

The different window shapes and sizes on the building's soft, curved facade look onto the surrounding landscape and add a dynamic feel. The windows are not randomly placed: the long, narrow rectangular slots outline the shape of the stairs inside and, in the library, rounded windows are large enough to double-up as reading spaces. Li Hu and Wenjing believe the rough plaster texture also adds to the beguiling character of the building, and such details pique the students' curiosity.

Stairs beside a long window in the Bibliotheatre (below left); a round window (below right); the windows and the skylights of the Bibliotheatre (opposite).

At first glance, the idiosyncratic shape of the Bibliotheatre hardly seems serious but, on closer inspection, the structure's complexity can be seen in combination with OPEN's concept of cultural engagement through architecture.

The physical model of the Bibliotheatre (below); a spatial diagram (opposite).

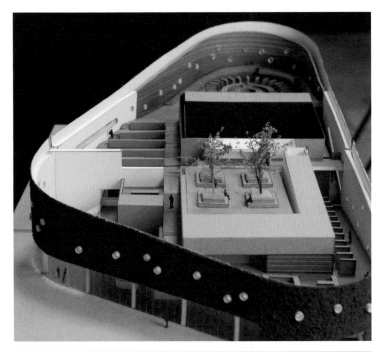

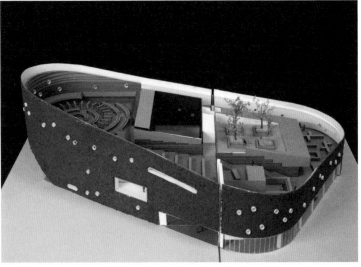

This marriage of library and theatre came from the architects' belief that the acts of reading and thinking, and of expression through performance are critical elements for education, and the broader community.

The distinctive qualities of these two programmes and their respective physical needs have influenced both the siting and the design of the building.

Near the secondary entrance to the campus, the main theatre access point is where the building is 'cut' diagonally to form a dramatic approach. From this point on the ground floor, there is a staircase leading visitors upstairs that can be conveniently accessed by parents and neighbours without disturbing the school.

The proscenium theatre and the Black Box theatre require no natural light and the most acoustic isolation, and, therefore, occupy the lower and central areas of the building, while the library is located above them. A loop of different reading spaces rises and falls according to the varying heights of the theatre below, creating a terraced spatial sequence that draws the eye upwards, invites visitors to explore every corner, and climaxes in a central reading area, surrounded by books and light. The design reflects the evolving role of libraries as hubs for other media and shared knowledge—and as a space to simply enjoy. What makes its spatial configuration all the more interesting is how it reveals itself slowly, with new sightlines and new connections as students walk through the building.

"By integrating and stacking these specialised spaces together, we were able to frame a book sanctuary, where every child can find a corner suitable for him or herself," Li Hu says.

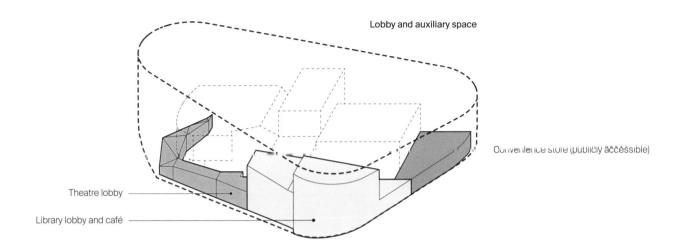

Lobby and auxiliary space

Convenience store (publicly accessible)

Theatre lobby

Library lobby and café

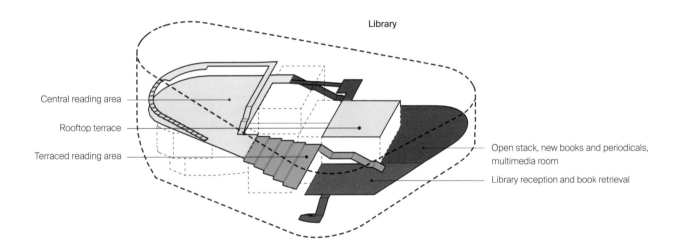

Library

Central reading area

Rooftop terrace

Terraced reading area

Open stack, new books and periodicals, multimedia room

Library reception and book retrieval

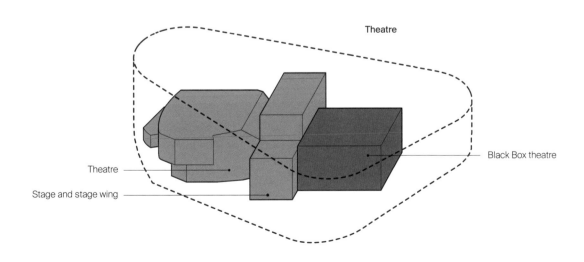

Theatre

Black Box theatre

Theatre

Stage and stage wing

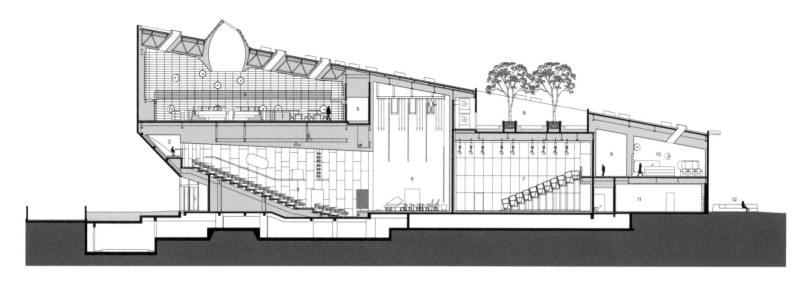

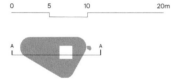

0   5   10   20m

Transverse Section A

1   Theatre lobby
2   Control room
3   Auditorium
4   Central reading area
5   Restroom
6   Stage
7   Black Box theatre
8   Rooftop terrace
9   Compact stacks
10 New books and periodicals
11 Convenience store open to the public
12 Rainwater-collection pond

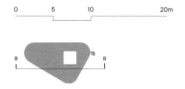

0   5   10   20m

Transverse Section B

1   Corridor
2   Library lobby
3   Indoor terrace
4   Open stacks reading room
5   Terraced reading area
6   Activity terrace
7   Staff office
8   Library reception
9   Book retrieval

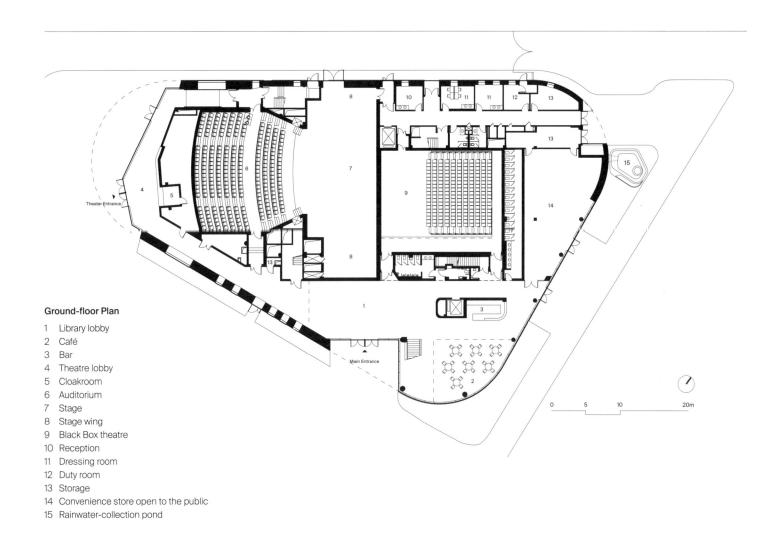

Ground-floor Plan

1 Library lobby
2 Café
3 Bar
4 Theatre lobby
5 Cloakroom
6 Auditorium
7 Stage
8 Stage wing
9 Black Box theatre
10 Reception
11 Dressing room
12 Duty room
13 Storage
14 Convenience store open to the public
15 Rainwater-collection pond

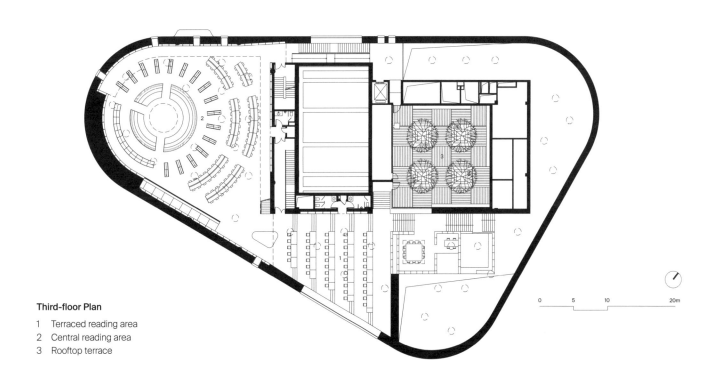

Third-floor Plan

1 Terraced reading area
2 Central reading area
3 Rooftop terrace

Reading can be introverted, highly personal, and a quiet activity, and so the architects have created several different, comfortable reading rooms for children and young adults. The sunken roof garden gives students a breath of fresh air too, with an outdoor reading area, when the weather permits.

However, in contrast, performing in a theatre is extroverted and exciting, and the Black Box inspires an intimacy for smaller audiences. The contrast of warm wooden panels and deep-blue walls results in a visually stimulating auditorium, and the ground-floor café also plays an important role. On school days, parents waiting to pick up their children can read or socialise there.

An outdoor terrace (above left); the theatre (above); the terraced reading space (left); the ground-floor café (right); the central reading area (overleaf).

In an era when the visual appeal of a library often dominates practical considerations, the architects focused on ensuring that students could reach the books. "Books are not a decoration," Li Hu says, and instead of traditional shelving and tables, they designed contrasting reading spaces, from tables and countertops to nooks and porthole-like window spaces, that make the reading experience fun.

"It is so interesting to see how the kids find a place that suits them," Wenjing observes.

The reading room, stepped between floors, gives students opportunities to interact, and elsewhere desks do double duty as bookshelves. This built-in flexibility is a major asset, and the school often uses the library as an extra classroom.

Light is essential to the design of the library, not only functionally but also to give form and rhythm. Forty-two skylights in the slanted roof infuse the central reading area with soft, natural daylight—and a giant oculus, four metres in diameter, illuminates the centre in an almost spiritual way, acting as the principal focus. "The diffused light produces a soft ambience that feels calm, so the kids find their books, then look for somewhere to sit and read," Wenjing explains.

In the theatre, the specially designed artificial lighting is used in a curious and dramatic way. On one side of the theatre wall, bulging to the exterior, there is a large and intriguing ear-canal-shaped installation that is lined with blue fabric and illuminated by a hidden light source, which attracts curious eyes. "I was thinking of Le Corbusier's chapel at Ronchamp and wanted something interesting that would extrude from the building," Li Hu says. Although the geometric volume has no particular function, it adds a dynamic form that is dominated by curved lines, and forms an emotional connection to the architectural experience.

The library reception (left); the theatre auditorium (opposite).

Despite its complex spatial
configuration, erecting the main,
prefabricated steel structure of
the Bibliotheatre only took about
two months as each large segment,
including the roof space frame,
was manufactured in a factory and
delivered to the site, where it was
then lifted and fixed into place.
Prefabrication meant that site and
foundation preparation could happen
while the components were being
built, and the on-site assembly of
precise steel elements was very quick,
which greatly shortened the critical
construction time.

The structural design also means
that there are no internal columns.
The cantilevered, prefabricated form
at the main entrance was the most
challenging to design, engineer,
and install. The architects wanted the
shape to follow the sloping geometry
of the seating above, and extend
onto a plaza, and so they worked
with experienced Chinese structural
engineers at the China Academy of
Building Research (CABR) to create
an "almost acrobatic entrance, like
the prow of a ship or the mouth of
a whale, which gives a sense of
lightness," Li Hu states, adding,
"but the cantilever is not just about
how it looks—the shape is an important
way to show the human scale of
the building."

The open stacks reading room (right);
the north side view at night (overleaf).

The Bibliotheatre is not what one might expect of a school library or theatre, and especially the contiguity of the two spaces in one building. The finished structure far exceeds what the client had hoped for, not only in terms of meeting the tight time constraints but also in thinking about how to integrate culture within the education system. For Li Hu and Wenjing, this integration is like nourishing soil to seedlings, and its importance cannot be overstated.

CHAPEL OF SOUND

In a mountainous, undeveloped valley in Chengde municipality, beside a dilapidated stretch of the Great Wall of China, a monolithic sculptural structure houses an open-air concert hall that doubles as a sanctuary, offering both shelter and contemplation within an organic form. Open to the public, it is part of a local-government plan to revitalise this remote rural area, which borders Beijing. However, since winters in this region are bitterly cold, the concert hall opens during the warmer months only.

The architects had previously worked closely with the client, Aranya cofounder Ma Yin, on the UCCA Dune Art Museum (see pp.24-59), which is hidden beneath the sands by the Bohai Sea in Qinhuangdao, so they knew that he would expect something out of the ordinary when he commissioned them again.

As with the earlier dune project, the architects were given a completely unrestricted brief and carte blanche to define the scope and scale—and location—of the structure. This opened up an unparalleled opportunity to explore ways to ensure their design would fit, and reinforce, the unusually desolate context in which it was situated.

"We were literally starting from scratch, since there was neither water nor electricity," Wenjing explains, "and the roads leading to the site in a deep-sided, secluded valley were rudimentary."

Apart from a small village, which has been abandoned as younger generations moved away to the cities to find work, the locale was completely undeveloped, yet the harsh beauty and powerful character of the mountainous landscape unique to this region in northern China struck Li Hu and Wenjing on their initial visit. Their first thought was to build as close as possible to the remnants of the Great Wall, but, having spent some time familiarising themselves with the site, they decided to retreat to a slightly flatter part of the valley, both for a broader angle of views and to respect the historical landmark.

The distant view (right); the rocks near the site that inspired the layered form of the building (opposite).

Rocks fascinate the two architects. They have always picked up local specimens wherever they go, and a rock collection from around the world is exhibited in their office. So, one of the first things they did at the start of this project was explore the interesting rock formations at the site. The mountainside geology has a particular characteristic, with layers of sediment deposited by the glacier that once moved through this valley.

They quickly realised that any attempt to embed architecture there would destroy the existing fragile topography. Instead, they decided "to translate that primitive quality into a building that would give the impression that a prehistoric boulder had fallen there."

"The most important thing in architecture is that it should always feel like it has a fundamental connection to the site," says Li Hu.

DESIGN CHALLENGES

Although they are accustomed to working in different environments and adapting their urban experience to rural areas, the couple had never worked anywhere quite like this. "Nothing that we took for granted existed, such as being able to get a good supply of commercial concrete mixture," the architects explain.

Working in such a remote area meant adapting their working habits—and being patient. The contractor built a small mixing facility nearby and, in the first year of construction, the building went up slowly, only reaching around seven metres above ground level. It picked up speed during the second year, once the workers were more experienced, and the unusual inverse conical form emerged.

There were no precise drawings of the valley, so one of the studio's young architects built a plaster model, by hand, on site, which was then replicated at larger scale in the Beijing office. Physical models became the basis for working on this project.

The site's remote location and challenging conditions made it difficult for the contractor as well. Li Hu and Wenjing turned to the experienced concrete expert, Mr Long, who was on the construction team that had worked with them at the UCCA Dune Art Museum. Working with concrete to create such a complex architectural form required Mr Long's specialist knowledge and experience, OPEN says, and it would have been almost impossible to complete the project without his supervision.

The hand-made plaster model (left); the building sitting at the bottom of the valley (opposite).

162

Right from the start, Li Hu and Wenjing wondered if they could try a new design methodology to create a space by sound, for sound.

"Many established typologies don't make sense anymore," they say, "and we felt that it was time to consider how to achieve a sensorial experience in a different way."

In their research, which underpins every OPEN project, they even discovered scenes of concerts being played in natural caves. "For us, it was deeply moving to see how nature cradles and amplifies music. Ultimately, music is as natural as life itself and has complemented human existence throughout history."

They also looked at the spiritual quality of music.

We liked the concept of a contemplative, chapel-like sanctuary, and how sound would reverberate in such a space. We did not want to be constrained by Western ideas of how a concert hall should look. When you have almost complete freedom to design, except for budgetary control of course, it is both exciting and dangerous. We feel it is very important to keep alert, keep questioning and re-examine everything.

Two sections through the building (opposite); an initial sketch by Li Hu (right).

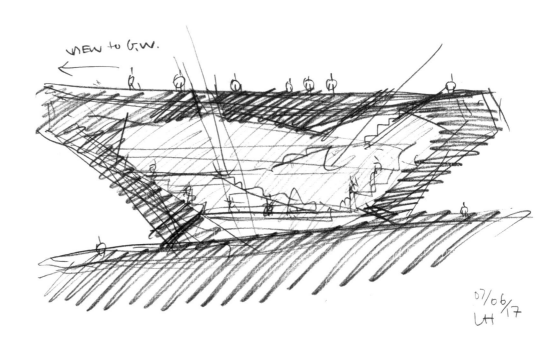

Study models.

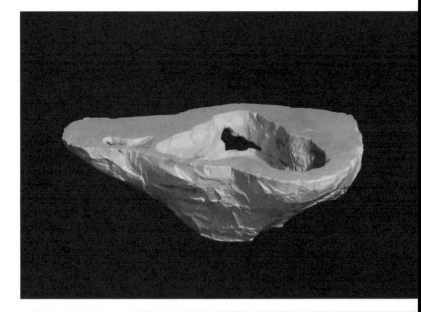

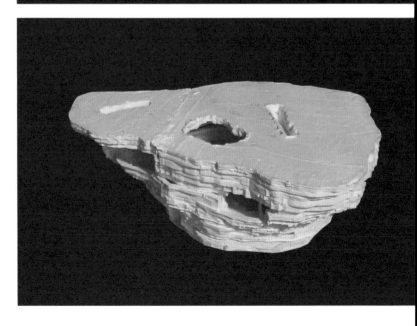

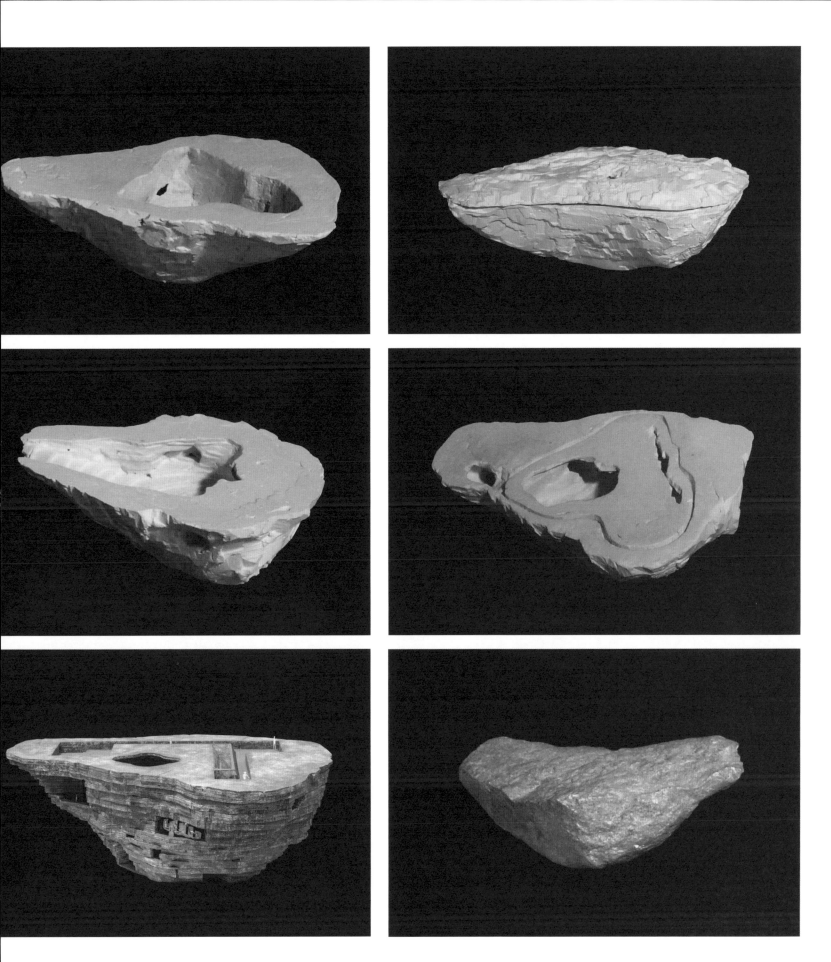

Part of their quest was to create an association between architecture, culture, and nature. Despite preconceived and often nostalgic ideas about the unique relationship that the Chinese have with nature and culture, Li Hu and Wenjing believe that there are fewer differences than similarities between the Chinese and other cultures in terms of how they live and their delight in cultural activities. "People everywhere want and need space to enjoy experiences. Human nature everywhere has a lot in common," they say. "In this way, we hope that architecture can serve to connect people across different cultures."

The name Chapel of Sound derives from a meeting held in March 2017 that Li Hu had with fellow architects Steven Holl and José Oubrerie, Professor Emeritus at the Knowlton School of Architecture at Ohio State University, when he was lecturing at Columbia University. Oubrerie, a protégé of Le Corbusier, was exhibiting his Chapel of Mosquitoes design project, and Li Hu was immediately taken with the expressive name and the qualities it evoked.

For the past decade, Li Hu has been lecturing on the environmental impact of overbuilding in China. He wanted to create something that would minimise both the excavation and the footprint of the building.

Their first sketches explored the idea of a completely open-air, rock-shaped amphitheatre.

"We didn't want to simply imitate a rock or make anything artificially, though," the architects point out, "so we designed a minimal and natural form that blends in with the environment, and yet is undeniably assertive and human."

Long after that design idea occured to him, Li Hu noticed with surprise that one of his favourite rocks, which he had found on his first visit to Delhi in 2008, was close in shape to the form he wanted for the Chapel of Sound.

Ma loved the initial concept but was concerned about the weather. The design was adjusted to add a partial cover with a roughly oval-shaped opening at the apex, much like the central oculus in the Pantheon's concrete dome.

"It may seem counter-intuitive to have a large opening, but ancient Roman architects knew how to drain water away to make their buildings work perfectly. We learned from them," Li Hu says. There is a system of carefully embedded drainage in the floor of the auditorium, so rainwater runs off quickly.

The large opening in the concert hall
(opposite).

"We always consider the emotional dimension of being inside a building," Li Hu observes. "Materiality and the effect of changing natural daylight arc difficult to express in images, so we start designing by thinking how it would feel to be inside, sheltered, and watching rain pouring down from the heavens. Now that it is built, the sights and sounds are amazing, and emphasise the sense of being protected inside a capsule within nature. We also enjoy sitting inside, listening to the wind and insects as their sounds are naturally amplified. Nature is part of the performance, orchestrating an ever-changing symphony. It really is a chapel of sound."

The double shell structure.

As soon as the initial proposal was approved, Li Hu and Wenjing knew they had to appoint the foremost engineers to retain the original shape and geometry of the complex 790-square-metre structure while creating a rustic, cave-like atmosphere. Arup was their choice: "They are specialists in unconventional engineering and worked hand-in-hand with us to fine-tune the complex geometry. Together, we devised the building as a double shell with a space between the inner and outer walls that operates like a truss."

The exposed concrete building facade (opposite); the concrete wall inside the concert hall (above); the semi-outdoor concert hall (overleaf).

The architects wanted the facade to take its cues from the local landscape and have a multifaceted feel, as if composed of layers of sediment. From their experience building the UCCA Dune Art Museum, they knew how difficult this would be, and decided simple formwork that looked like an abstraction of nature would be best.

"Concrete was a natural choice for its resilience in harsh outdoor environments," they recall, "but we didn't want regular concrete as it would look too bright and stand out glaringly in this environment." They experimented with different materials for mixing, such as the residue from local steel mills and iron furnaces, and crushed rocks from the valley, which were added as aggregates:

"Sediment proved to be a true inspiration. If you look closely at the concrete walls, you can see some reddish aggregates on the surfaces, and that comes from very special rocks in the valley."

Formally, each striation of the concrete cantilevers out from the layer immediately below to create the overall shape of an inverted cone. Structurally, this works similarly to the way in which traditional Chinese roofs achieve large cantilevers—layer by layer, incrementally reaching out.

The staircase between the inner and outer shells of the building (above); the main entrance and openings on the wall (opposite).

According to Li Hu, the greatest challenge was working out how to build the upper portion of the building, especially the front part where the cantilever is most dramatic. This is because a structural engineer's calculations are usually based on the strength of concrete when it has cured, not while it is still hardening. In this case, however, the on-site concrete master decided to significantly increase the scaffolding that supports the concrete at the frontal portion, to avoid sagging before the concrete had gained enough strength to support itself. The result was that the concrete was not deformed, despite the unusually extreme cantilever, which was a conclusion that Li Hu and Wenjing describe as "no less than a miracle."

Initially, openings through the building were designed by the architects to connect the interiors with the outdoor natural landscape, and acoustic engineers helped make them double as areas of sound absorption. Hard concrete surfaces reflect and refract sound, and the reverberation times in the chapel were meticulously calibrated through the manipulation of the building forms, and with the help of computer software, to produce the best possible quality of sound.

A performance taking place amid the scaffolding during construction (right); the concert-hall interior (bottom right and below); an acoustic diagram (opposite); the cantilevers layer by layer (overleaf).

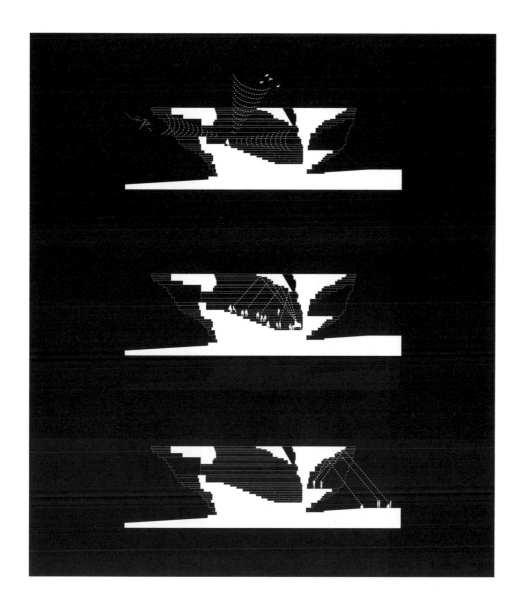

COLLECT

REVERBERATE

REFLECT

Despite numerous technical simulations, no one really knew how well the acoustics would work until the internal scaffolding had been removed. When Wenjing stood on the stage and clapped her hands, she knew immediately that it was a success: the sound was perfect. The acoustic engineer later confirmed this with his instruments.

"This is the challenge of architecture," Li Hu says. "You can design and imagine how it might be, and computer programmes are invaluable, but with sound and light you can never be absolutely sure until the very end."

Throughout the chapel, there are several viewing platforms, and the rear of the building has an outdoor stage that can be transformed into multiple configurations to host plays, concerts, and commercial events.

Li Hu and Wenjing believe that cultural architecture should not be designed to only accommodate large gatherings, and that the use of innovative engineering technology to create suspension and scale can instil a sense of wonder:

> We always consider different ways that people use space. The Chapel of Sound is dramatic, and it works in versatile ways and on multiple levels: indoors it seats up to 150 people on ringed tiers the shape of a human ear, but it still feels comfortable for one person alone in the space. It can accommodate outdoor performances, too, and an audience of up to 5,000 people sitting on the lawn.

We particularly like the spirit and honesty of the incongruity between the rough concrete surfaces and delicate, refined materials and details such as darkened bronze handrails and specially designed signage and custom lighting. Elsewhere, pre-weathered bronze panels and customised wash basins are installed in bathrooms, with part of the metal surfaces polished to a high, reflective shine, reminiscent of ancient Chinese mirrors.

At the rear of the stage, the architects have designed a fire trough for theatrical effects, "The stark concrete balances and sets off these special touches, evoking rather powerful sensations," Wenjing says.

A viewing platform (opposite left); a performance taking place in the concert hall (above); the outdoor stage (left); the bathroom (right); the main entrance (far right).

The Chapel of Sound is not just a distinctive, organic architectural form that feels at one with the environment: it also conveys something primordial and spiritual, which reflects the reality of nature itself.

Winding staircases lead to a rooftop platform that offers breathtaking panoramic views of the valley, and of the nearby Great Wall. While allowing daylight in, these openings also illuminate the performance space naturally and comfortably during the day.

"In the Chapel of Sound, even when no events are staged, there is natural harmony and space to reflect while surrounded by the sights and sounds of nature itself," the architects explain. People go there to experience something different, and to recognise that nature is both raw and beautiful.

The large opening on the roof (above); the front door (right); the staircase (opposite).

Li Hu and Wenjing are designing and building at a time when cultural institutions around the world are reinventing themselves to adapt to new social conditions. This is particularly so in China, where modernisation has arrived so fast. They firmly believe that cultural public buildings are not the sole preserve of the privileged, and feel fortunate that they can question and innovate even though the process may be difficult.

"That is why it is so important not to simply import existing typologies from developed countries: we have to adapt to new conditions, and the particularities of our own culture, and to design for the future," they say.

It is why we developed a new visual language, drawing on the local natural topography, which reimagines and creates new and unexpected uses of the space, so as to reinterpret not only the concert hall but also theatre itself. The objective is to create a building that is truly inspiring for the public.

"Sometimes, things seem to move at hyper speed in China and that often feels chaotic," Wenjing explains, "but the upside of this is that it is far easier to capture this generation's dynamic spirit, and to do something interesting and innovative."

The valley during winter (left);
a night view of the building (overleaf).

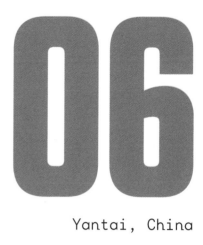

SUN
TOWER

Rising fifty metres above the sand, on a beach overlooking the Yellow Sea, the Sun Tower gives residents of Yantai's Fushan District, one of China's first Special Economic Zones, a new perspective on nature and the cosmos, as well as more earthly cultural pursuits, including a library, theatre, and café.

Yantai means 'smoke tower,' a name derived from the series of watchtowers built in the Ming dynasty that were also used to send smoke signals warning of impending attacks by pirates and raiders. In recent decades, scenic modern versions have become popular tourist attractions along China's coastline, but OPEN's new, undulating sculptural structure is more than a beacon to attract visitors and tourists to the natural beauty of the seaside.

It is a manifestation of the area's cultural revitalisation, from a fishing village founded more than 7,000 years ago to an influential port city in the late nineteenth century during the Qing dynasty, when there were considerable numbers of British, American, and German residents, into the industrial powerhouse it is today. The area is also home to the country's largest and oldest winery, Changyu.

The city's special economic status brought free-market-oriented economic policies, tax incentives, and flexible controls that have helped to transform it into a thriving hub for manufacturing cars, industrial machinery, electronics, and biopharmaceuticals. More recently, it has evolved from heavy industry to new and advanced technologies, and local government is increasingly turning its attention to improving the quality of life for residents by providing more outdoor leisure space and cultural activities.

A rendering of the Sun Tower and the plaza (opening page); the site and current cultural facilities in Yantai (right); site photos (opposite).

Li Hu recalls that it was OPEN's unusual design for the Chapel of Sound that caught the eye of Yantai's planning director, Mr Liu, who initially wanted to commission a tall, impressive, and symbolically powerful landmark on the city's beach. For reference, he mentioned Vessel, the unusual, forty-six-metre-high honeycomb structure, formed of 154 interlocking staircases and eighty landings, designed by British architect Thomas Heatherwick for Hudson Yards development in New York. Li Hu says:

> When it comes to design, especially iconic projects, Chinese people are very aware of what is happening in the design world. Sometimes we know more about what's happening elsewhere than they know about us.

OPEN was keen to move away from a single, dazzling statement monument toward one that would be useful, as well as impactful, and would do more than make a grandiose architectural gesture. Instead, Li Hu and Wenjing proposed an alternative design that would make its mark on the landscape, as well as contribute to the district's cultural infrastructure.

"It is not the first time in the course of a project that we have made changes to the original plan," Wenjing admits.

Mindful of the natural setting and Yantai's location on China's easternmost shore—it is known as one of the best cities from which to watch the sunrise—the architects envisioned something that would express an appreciation of the powerful natural marvels that occur at different times and seasons.

"We also wanted to recall ancient rituals around nature, long-forgotten in contemporary life, that are becoming relevant again in the face of today's global environmental crisis," they say.

The couple took notice of the growing need for and interest in public cultural programmes in Yantai, and began to develop the concept of an oceanside watchtower, where traditional observance could merge naturally with contemporary cultural life.

THE DESIGN CONCEPT

As with all their projects, the architects first researched the wider context of the site and the natural environment. The gentle half-moon bay is renowned for its calm waters, and forms an integral part of the city that lies directly to the south of the beach. The site is within a two-kilometre-long landscaped public park that stretches along the coast. Shortly before OPEN was commissioned, on the spot where the Sun Tower now stands, an illegally built high-rise apartment block was demolished, leaving only the structure's pile foundations.

"I think it is quite meaningful that something that was illegal, and intended solely for private use, has now been replaced by a building that is open to everyone," Li Hu says.

"This project was a rare case of a client who held the same values as we do of how a city should work and respect nature," Wenjing adds.

> In this case, quite a few people at the planning bureau have lived in and worked for the new district for almost two decades, and they truly understand it. They immediately embraced our idea that while the design could be ambitious and unorthodox, it should also be a civic project that engages with the city and achieves community goals, all while transforming the experience of the landscape.

Li Hu recalls that the basic design concept came to life after more than a dozen different schemes were tried out with the team. His very first sketch showed a simple, cone-shaped section with a theatre on the ground, a space in the middle, and a library at the top. When they tried this out in models, the closed-off, circular form did not look as impressive as they intended, so they went on looking. One day, they found what they had been searching for when Wenjing opened a 3D-printed model, which had been made in two pieces to show the internal structure, and it struck her that the model looked very intriguing with the building sliced open to face the sea.

The semicircular cone shape of the tower recalls the natural curved form and structure of seashells, as does the double layer of the inner and outer shells of the interior, which are connected by ramps. As Li Hu explains:

> When you build on a site like this, you are on the edge and humbled by the power of nature, and so it felt natural to think about the connection to the sun, moon, and stars, and to the relationship of light, space, and time. We immediately thought of the ancient human activities that honour nature, such as how Stonehenge in the United Kingdom was used as a place of sun worship.

Sketches by Li Hu (opposite).

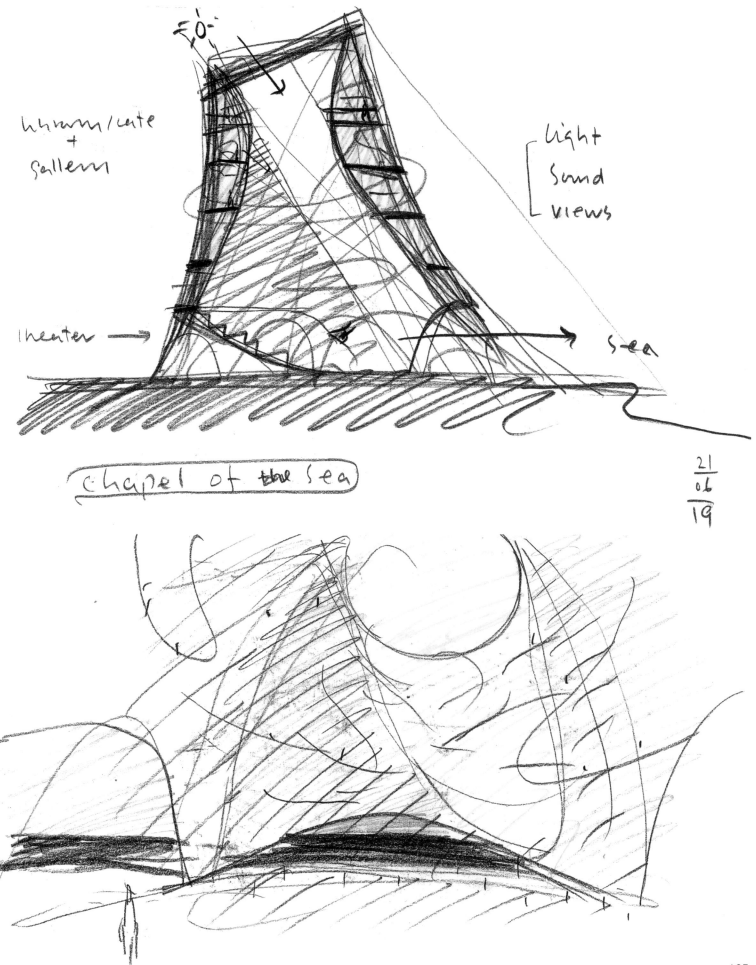

hmmm/cafe + gallery

light
sound
views

theater →

→ sea

chapel of ~~the~~ sea

21
06
19

The building's form is inspired by sunlight. During the spring and autumn equinoxes, and the summer and winter solstices, the movements of the sun, and the shadow it casts, are captured and marked by the building.

"Architecture becomes a stage for magnificent, natural sensations; a place to feel the power of nature, the meaning of time, and the mystery of the universe," say Li Hu and Wenjing.

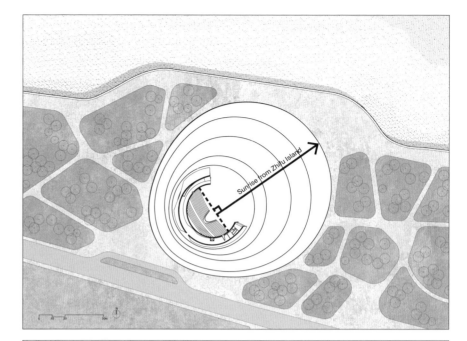

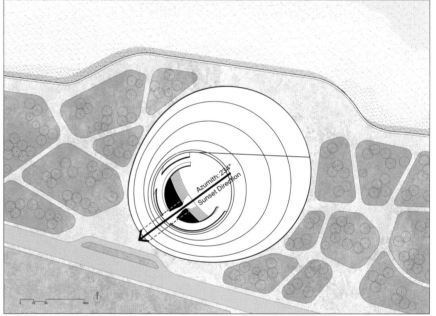

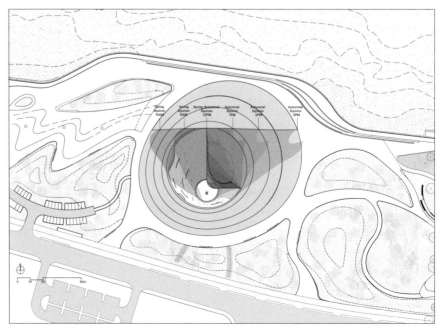

A summer solstice sunrise from Zhifu Island (top); a winter solstice sunset from the tunnel (centre); the linear movement of a shadow during the equinox (bottom).

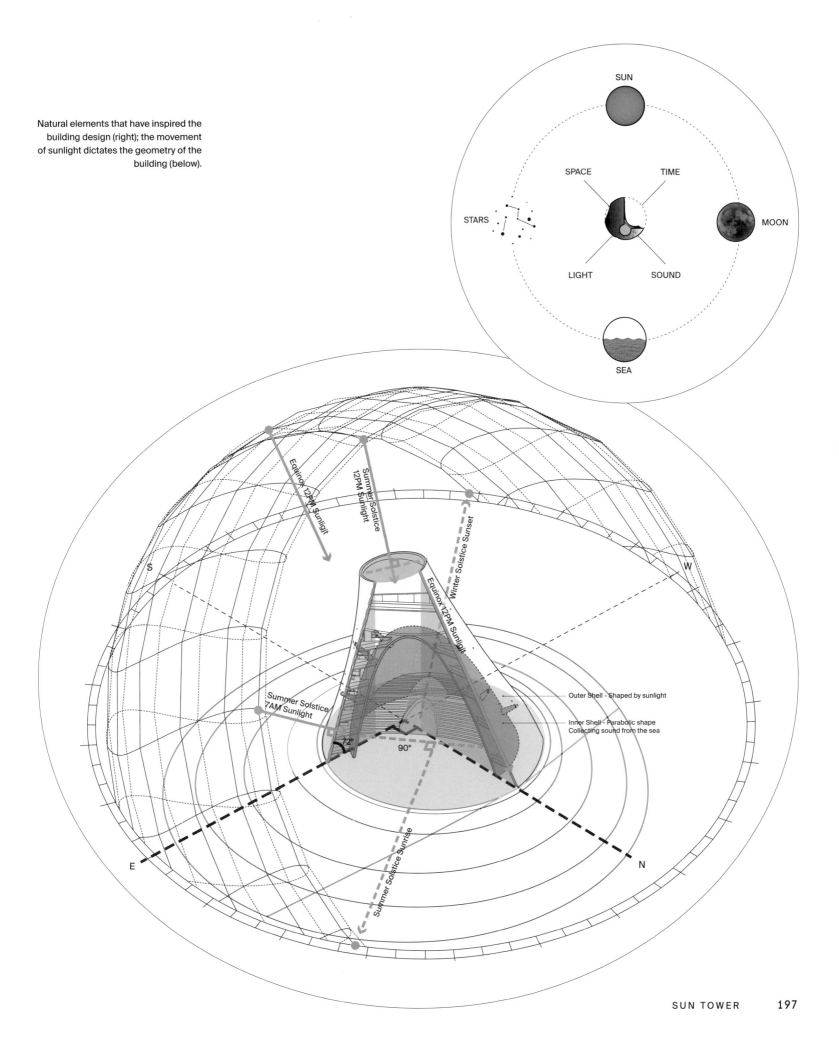

Natural elements that have inspired the building design (right); the movement of sunlight dictates the geometry of the building (below).

SUN

SPACE   TIME

STARS   MOON

LIGHT   SOUND

SEA

Equinox 12PM Sunligt

Summer Solstice 12PM Sunligt

Winter Solstice Sunset

Equinox 12PM Sunligt

S

W

Summer Solstice 7AM Sunlight

Outer Shell - Shaped by sunlight

Inner Shell - Parabolic shape
Collecting sound from the sea

72°

90°

E

Summer Solstice Sunrise

N

The building is set in a 11,435-square-metre plaza, and composed of three main, functional parts: a semi-outdoor theatre and café at the base; a winding exhibition space with eleven ocean lookouts in the middle; and, at the top, an airy, light-filled library, auditorium, and a 'phenomena space,' which is a part of the tower that remains intentionally empty so that the natural phenomena of the sky, ocean, sounds, and climate may be felt and observed.

The two layers of concrete that make up the tower's composite shells are connected and braced by horizontal slabs. The outermost layer is built with smooth white concrete that has been punctured by small rounded windows, which create a dramatic and starry pattern at night.

The inner layer has two shells: a large, parabolic lower shell that contains the semi-outdoor theatre and faces the sea, absorbing and amplifying the sounds of the ocean. The smaller, upside-down, upper shell houses the library and the phenomena space, and has panoramic vistas of the ocean and the sky above. The serene phenomena space has an oculus in its sweeping, concave ceiling, through which rainwater can enter and fill a pool during the summer. In winter, a fire is lit below the opening.

Visitors walk up a series of zigzagging ramps, which also function as digital multimedia exhibition spaces between the inner and outer layers. Educational exhibitions relate to nature and history, and merge with changing views of the ocean from balconies that are located at the turning point at each end of a ramp.

At the base of the tower, on the ground level, a stage area doubles as a plaza and completes the circular footprint shape of the tower above. The stage plaza has a shallow, cloud-shaped pool dotted with misting devices that transform it into a playful communal area when there is no performance. Surrounding the tower and radiating out in elliptical rings is the larger plaza, which first rises upwards for better views of the stage before dipping down again. On the ring at the ridge of the sloped, larger plaza, there is a semicircle of fountains, representing both the high and low tides of a day, and the twenty-four seasons of a Chinese lunar year. Both tidal and seasonal phenomena are linked to the phases of the moon, and highlighting them is a nod to the city's long history of oceanic culture, which is surprisingly rare in China.

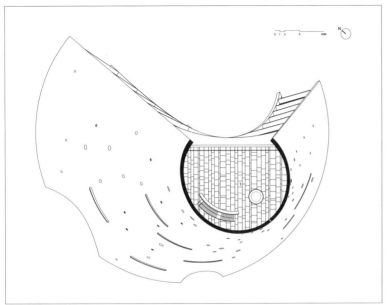

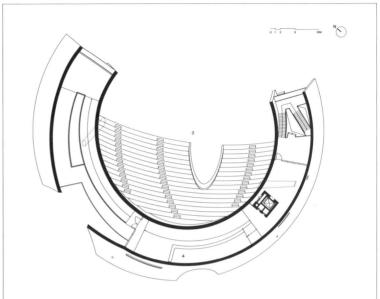

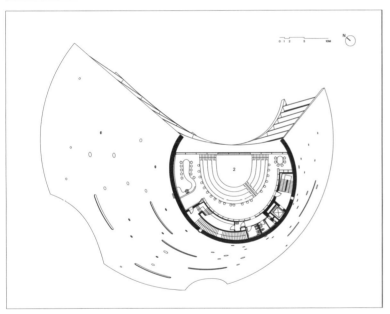

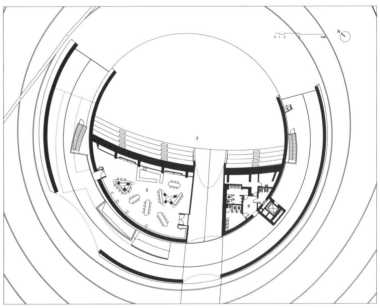

Phenomena space plan (top left)

1. Phenomena space

Library plan (above left)

2. Library

Gallery plan (top right)

3. Outdoor theatre
4. Gallery

Theatre plan (above right)

3. Outdoor theatre
5. Café
6. Public bathrooms

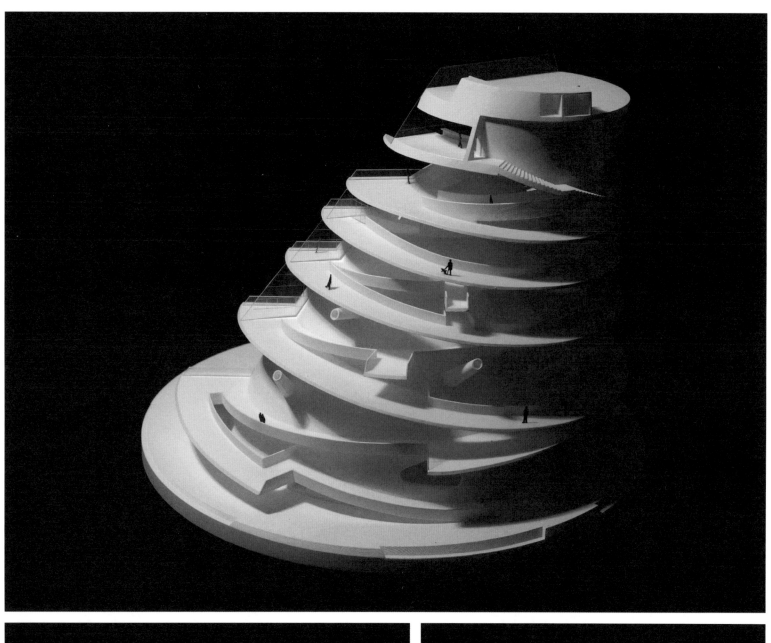

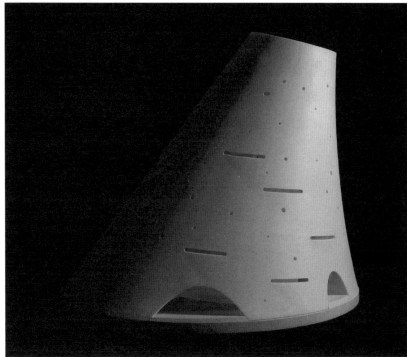

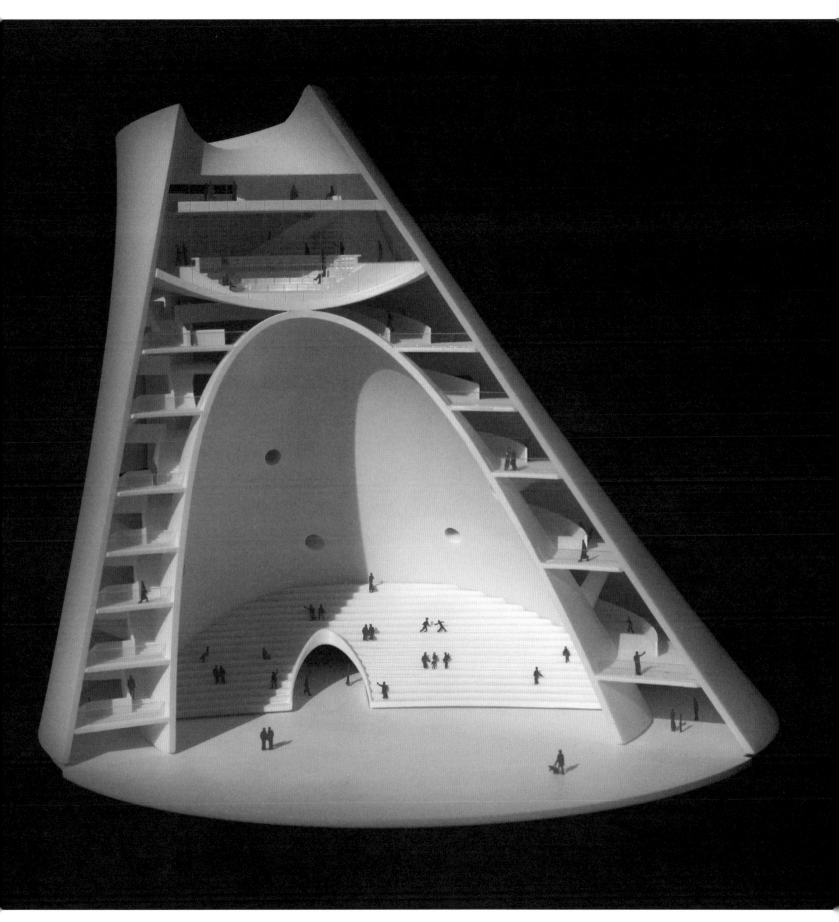

The physical model of Sun Tower.

ORIENTATION

Inspired by the universality of ancient architecture not only from China but from Egyptian, Greek, Roman, and Mayan cultures, which were built to worship the sun, Li Hu and Wenjing began to explore how they could make a connection between the tower, the sun, and the seasons—with light and shadow to be used as architectural materials.

"Nothing connects us more than the sun," Li Hu says. "The tower's geometry, openings, and shadows make it work like a big sundial."

The open cut of the Sun Tower positions the outdoor theatre to face the summer-solstice sunrise over the sea, in the direction of Zhifu Island. It was this ancient island, over 2,200 years ago, that the first emperor of China, Qin Shi Huang, is supposed to have visited three times in search of the elixir of immortality.

The entrance to the tower on the city-facing side is through an eighteen-metre-long tunnel that faces the solstice sunset. Chinese farmers have long adhered to the lunar calendar, and celebrate each equinox and solstice. Due to the building's unique geometry, the shadow of the equinox sunlight moves in a straight line across the plaza. The moving shadow and elliptical rings set into the plaza floor intersect at precise hours of the day, which are marked by plaques embedded in the pavement.

The equinox shadow line moving across the plaza (below); rendering of a view of the sunrise from the outdoor theatre at summer solstice (opposite).

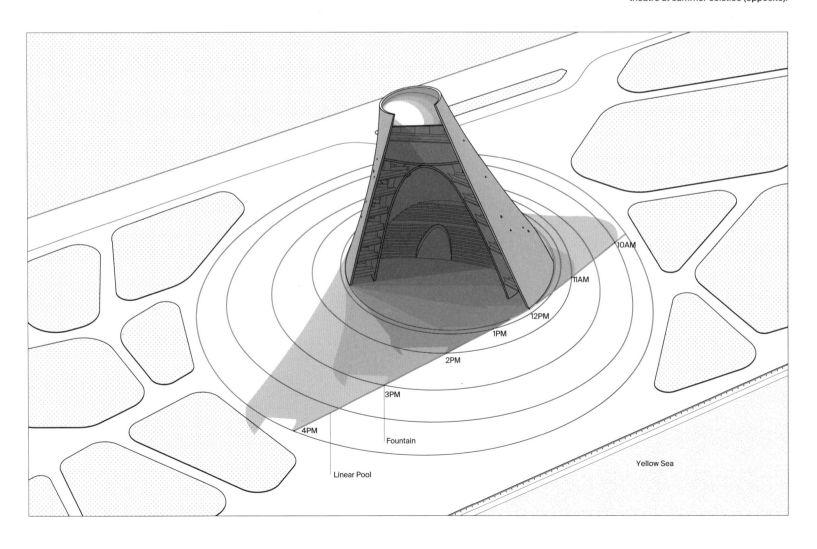

10AM
11AM
12PM
1PM
2PM
3PM
4PM
Fountain
Linear Pool
Yellow Sea

"We mirror the twenty-four seasons in the fountain in the plaza, which was designed using the Golden Ratio, a magic number, as appoximated by the Fibonacci sequence, found in nature, which, when applied to design, creates organic, balanced, and harmonious proportions," Li Hu explains.

Set against the building's urban presence and monumentality—the structure is a conscious counterpoint to the surrounding beach—the interior is a surprisingly intimate spatial sequence: as the plaza and vertical promenade zigzag upward, visitors discover the tower's many faces and expressions, as well as the two intentionally juxtaposed parallel worlds of digital exhibitions and ocean views.

The ocean-facing side of the building is the most open and active facade, reflecting Li Hu's and Wenjing's desire to create an easily accessible landmark that has a soul.

Due to the gentle gradient of the beach, low tides retreat far back on the seabed, and so the plaza is always dry, even at high tide.

"Architecture is a measurement. Capturing the moment and framing the connection is how we bring order to things. Without measurements, we can't feel or count or mark," Li Hu explains.

Li Hu and Wenjing see the tower as a pedagogical device, one that informs and connects a visitor to the world around them. It does this by creating a visual relationship with the sea, which orientates them as they walk upwards, along sinuous ramps, becoming increasingly immersed in the silent, spiritual oceanscape. The tower is also an exhibition space, providing information about nature, the global energy crisis, and marine life.

A rendering of the building during the winter as it faces the sea (opposite top); an image of the entrance and ramp (opposite bottom); a rendering of the phenomena space (left); an image of the space between the upper and lower shells (bottom left); a rendering of the digital gallery (below).

"We wanted to create a bold building with meaning and function, and not a hollowed-out structure used for shock and awe, and each step is very deliberately designed so that, gradually, you open your heart and your mind to the ocean and cosmos in this ascent," Wenjing explains.

MATERIALITY

The concrete mock-ups of Sun Tower

The material used in the Sun Tower is simple—mainly white concrete. When employed on such a grand scale, white concrete would normally be quite expensive since it requires a specific combination of cement, aggregates, and sands. Serendipitously a pristine, white, and more affordable stone was available locally, and the architects experimented with it in different concrete mixtures and applications, and were able to form a variety of textures, from smooth to wood-imprinted surfaces.

To echo the structure and haptic qualities of a giant seashell, Li Hu and Wenjing used formwork to create interesting textures and empty spaces between the upper shell-like bowl and the lower shell of the theatre.

For all its dramatic, imposing architectural form, the real artistry in the building may be its fresh expression of urbanism. The Sun Tower is a distinct feature in a landscape that gives the city its special character, and the building also transcends its initial function as an exhibition space for art: its spiritual connection with the universe inspires creative interactions between the public and the landscape.

Every angle, measurement, and form is determined by its alignment with the Earth's axis. The light shining through windows and openings in the gigantic curvaceous shell suggests the glow of a lantern, as visitors climb instinctively up the tower.

Sitting on the steps of the viewing deck, under the dramatic curved parabolic shell, visitors can gaze at the distant ocean, framed by the building's dramatic arch.

"Architecture aligned with the axis of the Earth pays tribute to nature, and the sounds of nature breathing echo gently, reminding us we are alive," Wenjing explains.

A rendering of the library and lookouts (opposite top); a rendering of the library interior (opposite bottom); the building seen at night from the city (left).

Since museums need considerable resources, Li Hu and Wenjing envisioned a 'light' institution, which would require minimal staff and maintenance, as well as reduced programming costs from the addition of inbuilt digital screens and projections. They also foresaw a flexible institution that would attract a mix of people, from art and nature lovers to students. So the structure offers many combinations of passages and circuits, and the layout of the interior and plaza are ideal for holding an event or enjoying views of the ocean. The small library, with its curated collection of books on nature, is also designed for drama and poetry readings.

There is an elevator for anyone who needs it, and an outdoor staircase for quick access to the top, but the architects hope that most visitors will go up the comfortably sloped ramps and enjoy the alternating views of the city and the ocean, as well as the multimedia exhibitions. They believe that the climb up to the summit will provide a new and worthwhile experience.

In this project, Li Hu and Wenjing venture into a more spiritual dimension of design, exploring the universal power of architecture.

"Architecture becomes a stage for the magnificent natural world," they say, "where we can feel the power of nature, the meaning of time, and the mystery of our universe."

AN OPEN MANIFESTO

Li Hu + Huang Wenjing
Founding Partners of OPEN Architecture

The world is a complex system of elements,
constantly interacting and in flux.
Architecture is a vessel, a medium through which to interpret
increasingly complex issues at work.
It is a means to gather and connect,
in meaningful ways.

We have been patiently in search of
architecture that is OPEN,
which establishes intricate relationships between
the forces in this confluence.
Architecture that connects us with people—to meet, exchange, and share.
Architecture that connects us with nature—trees and birds, sea and land, air and light.
Architecture that connects us with ourselves.

These connections speak to how we imagine
our very human existence, among ourselves, and others of the world.
In the moments of dialogue we share,
new knowledge and friendships form, new ideas and reflections emerge.

To arrive at this point is a journey of discovery.
For each project, there is a new beginning.
We are eyes searching for hidden signs, ears catching imperceptible voices.
We must discover, within each project, what is really needed,
what is called for, and what must become.

All existing formulas, languages, and all that is taken-for-granted,
must be reconsidered and challenged,
until we arrive at the unfamiliar territory of new discoveries.

We are moving away from the established, the contemporary, and the expected,
away from image-making and smooth operations.
Our work starts from within, the core, the inside;
and then we carve our way out, with imagination.
Architecture must be radical, yet still deeply poetic.
It must ask radical questions, seek radical solutions,
enact change, and ask for engagement,
heighten awareness, and demand reflection.

Poetry exists in the sublime and mystical,
in the experience of the passing of time, in the sensing of minute details.
Architecture touches life in and around itself.
It creates the depth through which space and time are experienced.

Architecture must be authentic and grounded,
simple and relaxed. It must protect its own integrity,
so that those inhabiting it can be themselves with dignity.

Architecture must be modest.
Consuming minimal resources, minimising impact on natural surroundings,
it encourages generosity, in mind and in action,
to include, protect, care, and nurture.

Architecture need not be entirely completed.
It should leave space for improvisation
and the inevitability of future change.
Architecture must also be
a little humorous, surprising, and informal.

In the end, architecture will speak for itself,
have its own life,
tell its own stories.

This is the architecture of OPEN.

PROJECTS TIMELINE

Flexible and Reusable Building System V1.0
Beijing
11/2012–08/2013

HEX-SYS
Guangzhou
04/2014–07/201?

Sky City
Wuhan
09/2011–08/2020

Beehive Dormitory
Fuzhou
10/2009–12/2009

TANK SHANGHAI
Shanghai
01/2013–03/2019

Studio-X Beijing
Beijing
03/2009–09/2009

Gehua Youth and Cultural Centre
Qinhuangdao
01/2012–07/2012

Venice Biennale
China Pavilion
Outdoor Installation
Venice, Italy
02/2014–06/2014

Red Line Park
Beijing/Shenzhen
01/2008–12/2009

Mobile Joy Station
Beijing
09/2012–11/2012

2008 2009 2010 2011 2012 2013 2014

2nd Ring 2049
Beijing
04/2009–10/2009

Mount Theatre Competition
Nyon, Switzerland
10/2012–11/2012

BCU Campus Ce
Beijing
03/2014–01/201?

Metro Valley
New Delhi, India
06/2008–10/2009

Stepped Courtyards
Fuzhou
12/2011–08/2014

Tsinghua Ocean Centre
Shenzhen
11/2011–12/2016

Beijing No.4 High School Fangshan Campus
Beijing
04/2010–08/2014

PINGSHAN PERFORMING ARTS CENTRE
Shenzhen
03/2013–10/2019

212

Lakeshore Peaks
Chengdu
06/2016–

Sea Art Museum
Qinhuangdao
07/2015–

Lake Art Centre
Kunming
12/2020–

Shenzhen Maritime
Museum Competition
Shenzhen
06/2020–08/2020

Foreign Book Centre
Beijing
01/2021–

Longhua Museum and Library Competition
Shenzhen
07/2015–10/2015

CHAPEL OF SOUND
Chengde
05/2017–08/2021

The New Normal at UCCA
Beijing
01/2017–03/2017

ZTE Headquarters Base Competition
Shenzhen
05/2018–06/2019

Suzhou Shanfeng Campus Centre
Suzhou
03/2020–

2016　2017　2018　2019　2020　2021　2022

Pudong Art Museum Competition
Shanghai
11/2015–06/2016

Soul of City
Verona, Italy
02/2017–09/2017

Mars Case
Beijing
11/2017–09/2018

Netdragon Library Complex
Fuzhou
04/2019–06/2020

Taihu Camp
Wuxi
08/2020–

UCCA DUNE ART MUSEUM
Qinhuangdao
07/2015–10/2018

SUN TOWER
Yantai
06/2019–

Beijing HACC Arts Centre
Beijing
01/2018–

SHANGHAI QINGPU PINGHE INTERNATIONAL SCHOOL
Shanghai
11/2016–08/2019

Nanshan Commune
Shenzhen
08/2019–

Tiantai Art Museum
Tsingtao
10/2020–

PROJECTS MAP

Nyon, Switzerland

Venice, Italy
Verona, Italy

New Delhi, India

Mount Theatre
Soul of City
Venice Biennale China Pavilion

Metro Valley

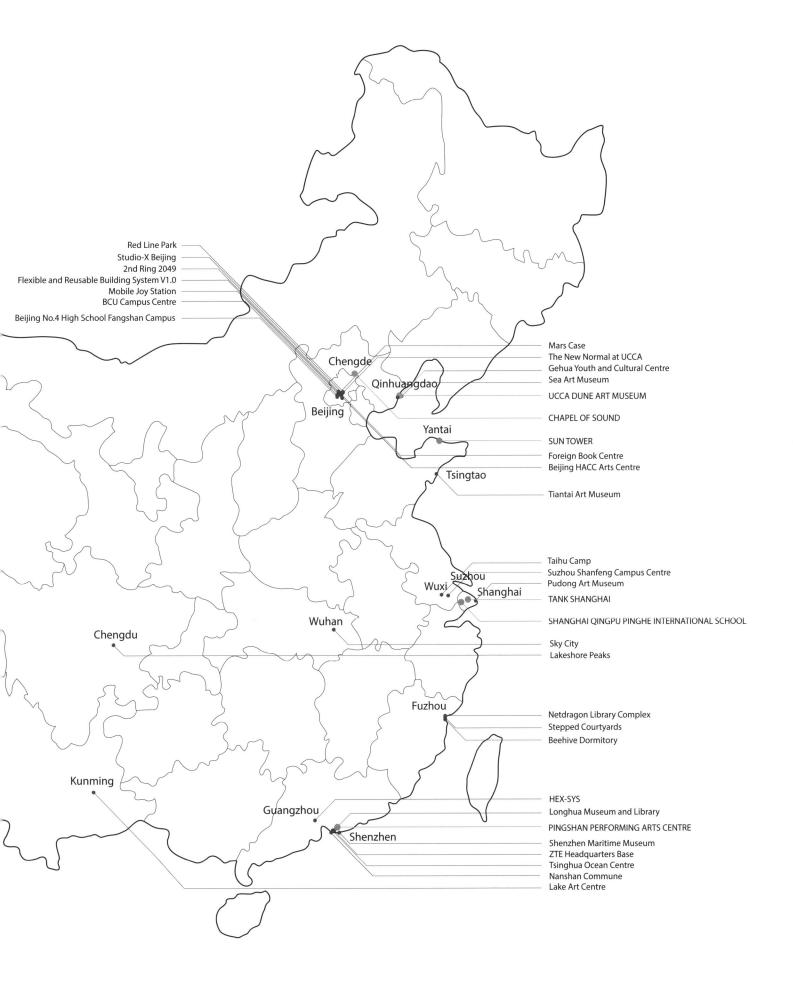

Red Line Park
Studio-X Beijing
2nd Ring 2049
Flexible and Reusable Building System V1.0
Mobile Joy Station
BCU Campus Centre
Beijing No.4 High School Fangshan Campus

Chengde
Qinhuangdao
Beijing
Yantai
Tsingtao

Mars Case
The New Normal at UCCA
Gehua Youth and Cultural Centre
Sea Art Museum
UCCA DUNE ART MUSEUM
CHAPEL OF SOUND
SUN TOWER
Foreign Book Centre
Beijing HACC Arts Centre
Tiantai Art Museum

Suzhou
Wuxi
Shanghai
Wuhan
Chengdu

Taihu Camp
Suzhou Shanfeng Campus Centre
Pudong Art Museum
TANK SHANGHAI
SHANGHAI QINGPU PINGHE INTERNATIONAL SCHOOL
Sky City
Lakeshore Peaks

Fuzhou

Netdragon Library Complex
Stepped Courtyards
Beehive Dormitory

Kunming
Guangzhou
Shenzhen

HEX-SYS
Longhua Museum and Library
PINGSHAN PERFORMING ARTS CENTRE
Shenzhen Maritime Museum
ZTE Headquarters Base
Tsinghua Ocean Centre
Nanshan Commune
Lake Art Centre

PROJECTS DETAILS

01 UCCA DUNE ART MUSEUM

PROJECT FACTS

Design Year: 2015–2018
Client: Aranya
Operator: UCCA Center for Contemporary Art
Programme: reception, café, exhibition spaces, outdoor exhibition, roof terrace
Building Area: 930 sqm
Location: Qinhuangdao, China

CREDITS

Architectural and Interior Design: OPEN
Local Design Institute: CABR Technology Co., Ltd.
Lighting Design: Tsinghua University X Studio + OPEN
Signage Design: Beijing Trycool Culture and Art Development Co., Ltd.

02 TANK SHANGHAI

PROJECT FACTS

Design Year: 2013–2019
Client: Shanghai West Bund Development Group + Tank Shanghai
Programme: art galleries, event spaces, restaurant, café, live music club, museum offices, art storage
Building Area: 10,845 sqm
Site Area: 47,448 sqm
Location: Shanghai, China

CREDITS

Architectural and Interior Design: OPEN
Local Design Institute: Tongji Architectural Design Group
Landscape Design: OPEN + Beijing EDSA Orient Planning & Landscape Architecture Co., Ltd.
Lighting Consultant: Shanghai Ming Chi Architecture and Engineering Co., Ltd.
Signage Design: One Thousand Times

03 PINGSHAN PERFORMING ARTS CENTRE

PROJECT FACTS

Design Year: 2013–2019
Client: Pingshan District Government, Shenzhen
Project Management: China Merchants Property Development Co., Ltd.
Programme: 1,200-seat theatre, 150-seat Black Box theatre, dance studio, instrument and choral rehearsal rooms, café and restaurant
Building Area: 23,542 sqm
Site Area: 14,302 sqm
Location: Shenzhen, China

CREDITS

Architectural and Interior Design: OPEN
Local Design Institute: Shenzhen Aube Engineering Design Consultant Co., Ltd.
Curtain Wall Consultant: Schmidlin Façade Consultancy
Theatre/Acoustic Consultant: JH Theatre Architecture Design Consulting Company
Stage Equipment Consultant: Zhejiang Dafeng Architecture and Decoration Co., Ltd.
Lighting Consultant: United Artists Lighting Design Consultants
Landscape Design: Aube + OPEN
Signage Design: Han Jiaying Studio

04   PINGHE BIBLIOTHEATRE

PROJECT FACTS

Design Year: 2016–2020
Client: Shanghai Tixue Education and Technology Co., Ltd.
Programme: 500-seat theatre, 200-seat Black Box theatre, library, café
Building Area: 5,372 sqm
Site Area: 2,312 sqm
Location: Shanghai, China

CREDITS

Architectural and Interior Design: OPEN
Local Design Institute: Shanghai Yuangou Architects and Consultants
Structural and MEP Engineers: CABR Technology Co., Ltd.
Curtain Wall Consultant: CABR Technology Co., Ltd.
Theatre/Acoustic Consultant: Shanghai Net Culture Development Co., Ltd.
Lighting Consultant: Shanghai Modern Architecture Decoration Environmental Design Research Institute Co., Ltd.
Landscape Design: OPEN
Signage Design: Beijing Trycool Culture and Art Development Co., Ltd.

05   CHAPEL OF SOUND

PROJECT FACTS

Design Year: 2017–2021
Client: Aranya
Size: 790 sqm
Location: Chengde, China

CREDITS

Architectural and Interior Design: OPEN
Structural & MEP Engineers: Arup
Lighting Consultant: Ning Field Lighting Design
Theatre/Acoustic Consultant: JH Theatre Architecture Design Consulting Company
Landscape Design: Guangzhou Turen Landscape Planning Co., Ltd.
Signage Design: OPEN

06   SUN TOWER

PROJECT FACTS

Design Year: 2019-2023
Client: Yantai Yeda Industrial Co., Ltd
Programme: Ocean watchtower, semi-outdoor theatre, digital gallery, library, meditation space
Building Area: 3,885 sqm
Site Area: 9,854 sqm
Location: Yantai, China

CREDITS

Architectural and Interior Design: OPEN
Structural and MEP Engineers: Arup
Lighting Consultant: Ning Field Lighting Design
Fire Fighting Consultant: CABR Technology Co., Ltd.
Scenographer: dUCKS scéno
Landscape Design: OPEN

Chen Hao, see following pages: 89 (bottom), 128, 134 (top), 138 (top right), 139, 148 (top right).

INSAW Image, see following pages: 62–63, 76, 77, 80–81, 88 (bottom), 90–91, 93 (left).

JJY Photo, see following pages: 67, 68, 92 (top left, bottom).

Jonathan Leijonhufvud, see following pages: front cover, 2–3, 98, 105, 106, 107, 108 (left), 109 (bottom right), 112–113, 114 (bottom left), 116, 117, 118, 119, 120 (left), 121 (top right, bottom), 122, 126–127, 130–131, 142, 143, 148 (top left, bottom), 150–151, 152, 154–155, 158, 160, 163, 169, 170–171, 174–175, 176, 177, 180–181, 182, 183, 184, 185, 188–189

James Leng, see following pages: 36 (bottom), 44 (top left, bottom left).

Ma Nan, see following pages: 52, 53.

Ni Nan, see following pages: 37, 50, 51, 55, 186–187.

OPEN, see following pages: 13, 27, 28, 29, 33, 34, 35, 41 (top left), 49, 50, 51, 56, 66, 70, 71, 72, 73, 75 (top), 83, 85, 93 (right), 100, 102, 103, 104, 144, 145, 146, 147, 161, 162, 164, 165, 166–167, 173, 178 (top right, bottom right), 179, 190, 192, 193, 195, 196, 197, 199, 200, 201, 202, 203, 204, 205, 206 (top left, top right), 208, 209, 214–215.

Kris Provoost, see following page: 120 (right).

Tank Shanghai, see following page: 95.

Tian Fangfang, see following pages: 36 (top), 44 (top right), 45 (bottom), 48, 51, 54 (bottom left), 69, 88 (top).

UCCA Center for Contemporary Art, see following pages: 58–59.

Wu Qingshan, see following pages: 24, 30-31, 38-39, 41 (top middle), 42, 43, 45 (top, middle), 46-47, 57, 60, 64-65, 74, 75 (bottom), 78, 79, 82, 84, 86-87, 89 (top right), 133, 134 (bottom), 135, 136-137, 138 (bottom), 140, 141, 149 (bottom right), 153, 156-157, 178 (bottom left), 206 (bottom left), 207, back cover.

Xia Zhi, see following pages: 51, 132.

Zaiye Studio, see following pages: 40, 41 (top right), 50, 54 (top right), 172.

Zeng Tianpei, see following pages: 108 (right), 109 (bottom left), 110, 111, 114–115, 123, 124–125.

Zhu Qingyan see following pages: 96–97.

LI HU

Li Hu graduated from Tsinghua University, Beijing, in 1996 before receiving his Master of Architecture degree from Rice University, Houston, Texas, in 1999.

In 2000, Li Hu began working at Steven Holl Architects in New York, becoming a partner in 2005. He founded and directed SHA's Beijing office until he left the practice in 2010. While at SHA, he worked on cultural, institutional, large-scale, mixed-use schemes, and was responsible for several major award-winning projects in Asia, such as the Linked Hybrid in Beijing and the Vanke Center in Shenzhen.

Li Hu is a visiting professor at the Tsinghua University School of Architecture and Central Academy of Fine Arts, Beijing. From 2009 to 2014, he was the director of Columbia University GSAPP's Studio-X Beijing, and often speaks at academic conferences and universities worldwide. He is also a frequent juror and curator for important international design competitions and exhibitions.

HUANG WENJING

Huang Wenjing graduated from Tsinghua University, Beijing, in 1996 before completing a master's degree at Princeton University, New Jersey, in 1999. She is a licensed architect in New York State and member of the American Institute of Architects.

Wenjing worked for seven years at Manhattan-based Pei Cobb Freed & Partners, on projects such as the expansion of the OECD headquarters in Paris. In 2006, she left Pei Cobb Freed to focus on OPEN, where a close collaboration with Li Hu has allowed them to explore the symbiotic relationship between people, the built environment, and nature.

Wenjing is a visiting professor at Tsinghua University, the Central Academy of Fine Arts, Beijing, and the University of Hong Kong.

OPEN

OPEN was founded in New York in 2006, initially as a space for experimentation and research, where Li Hu and Wenjing explored their joint interests. After moving back to China, the couple established their Beijing office in 2008. It was in 2010, after the office won its first important commission through competition—the Garden School in Beijing—that Li Hu left Steven Holl Architects to focus on OPEN. Since then, OPEN has secured many more major commissions, gaining recognition in China and worldwide.

OPEN's work has been widely published and frequently exhibited around the world, including in the Chicago Architecture Biennial, Venice Biennale, and London Design Museum, and collected by the Museum of Modern Art in New York and M+ Museum in Hong Kong.

Recent awards include the 2021 AR Future Project Awards (UK), 2020 London Design Museum's Beazley Designs of the Year Nominee (UK), 2019 LEAF Awards (EU), 2019 P/A Awards (US), 2018 AIA Education Facility Design Award of Excellence (US), 2017 Iconic Awards Best of Best (Germany), among many others.

Li Hu and Huang Wenjing have written three books about OPEN: *OPEN Questions* (2018), *Towards Openness* (2018), and *OPEN Reaction* (2015). They were both included in *50 under 50: Innovators of the 21st Century*, a 2015 book on architects, designers, and artists from around the world.

ACKNOWLEDGEMENTS

OPEN

Creating a book is no less complicated than creating a building. We would like to thank Catherine Shaw wholeheartedly for her passion and patience in all her conversations with us, when she listened to the stories behind each project, and our views on architecture and the world. She retells it all from her own perspective, and with acute sensitivity after her years of immersion in the cultural life that connects East and West so closely.

Our sincere gratitude goes to Rizzoli and the editorial team at Akkadia Press, for their encouragement and insights, and the creative design of Elizabeth Ballantyne, which resonates with the energy and spirit of our projects. The coordination that has gone into this book happened magically in four cities in Asia and Europe, mostly during the unprecedented COVID-19 pandemic. While the invisible virus wrought havoc, it also shed light on things that are too often ignored, such as how people long to connect with each other and with the world—which we always try to do in our architecture. We hope this book will illuminate the post-pandemic cultural sphere.

Only six projects are included in this book, and six is not a lot, but the effort expended over the past six years that it took to complete these projects has been considerable and constant. We have been lucky enough to meet the most wonderful clients who believed in us, gave us freedom to imagine, and who have supported us throughout each serious undertaking.

None of these projects were easy to build. In the end, the builders were very much a part of the work, and they, too, have influenced the results.

Incubating and nurturing a project to fruition requires untold hours of creative but sometimes tedious work from many collaborators. Besides OPEN's own passionate team of architects and designers, there are also brilliant engineers, consultants, and local architects who challenged themselves with these difficult tasks. To all those individuals whose resilience and enthusiasm helped to get the work done so magnificently, we owe a huge debt of gratitude.

We are also really grateful to Martino Stierli for our discussion, and for his insights on topics that are very important to us. Last, but not least, we would like to thank Aric Chen for his generous foreword, and, more importantly, for our deep-rooted friendship and his astute observations and critiques over the past decade—and, hopefully, for many more in the future.

CATHERINE SHAW

Ever since I moved to Hong Kong in the early 1990s to work as an urban planner, I have enjoyed a privileged, ringside seat from which to observe China's dramatic economic, social, and architectural transformations. I am indebted to Li Hu and Wenjing for generously adding their own personal perspectives over our many hours of conversation. Their joint, indefatigable spirit is driven by questioning the role in society played by the institutions they design, and as I have learned about each of their projects, I have also discovered more about the entire world. This has been an ideal opportunity to stand back and reflect on the many changes that have taken place over the past three decades, and I am particularly appreciative for those valuable insights.

I am especially grateful to the editorial team at Akkadia Press: to Anne Renahan, the director, and Bryony Quinn, who brought her skills and rigour to editing the texts, and I owe a special debt of gratitude to the unwavering support and critical professional advice of Clare Wadsworth.

I am indebted to Francesco Baragiola Mordini at Rizzoli for his patience and guidance, and his team, which includes Alexia Casals Leppo, Costanza de Bellegarde, Meri Micalizzi, Sara Saettone, and Cecilia Curti, for their expert assistance. I also wish to express my thanks to the book's designer, Elizabeth Ballantyne, for her wonderful work, and Rizzoli Art Director Dario Tagliabue for his oversight of the design process. I am also most grateful to OPEN's Director of Communications, Chen Cheng, for her professional assistance throughout.

Above all, and as always, I am thankful for the wholehearted encouragement of my husband Alistair and our children Alexandra and Francesca, and my sister Moira.

ISBN: 978-88-918319-5-8

2021 2022 2023 2024 / 10 9 8 7 6 5 4 3 2 1

First edition: March 2022

Project manager: Anne Renahan, Akkadia Press
Project communications: Chen Cheng, OPEN
Design and layout: Lizzie Ballantyne, Lizzie B Design, Akkadia Press
Editor: Bryony Quinn, Akkadia Press
Proofreader: Ian McDonald, Akkadia Press

This volume was printed at O.G.M. SpA
Via 1ª Strada, 87 - 35129 Padova
Printed in Italy

Visit Rizzoli online:
Facebook.com/RizzoliNewYork
Twitter: @Rizzoli_Books
Instagram.com/RizzoliBooks
Pinterest.com/RizzoliBooks
Youtube.com/user/RizzoliNY
Issuu.com/Rizzoli

Visit OPEN online:
Instagram.com/open.architecture
www.openarch.com